SPELLBOUND TWO

POWELL HAYLLAR SADLER

M

First published 1978 by
THE MACMILLAN COMPANY OF AUSTRALIA PTY LTD
107 Moray Street, South Melbourne 3205
12 Berry Street, North Sydney 2060

Associated companies in
London and Basingstoke, England
New York Dublin Johannesburg Delhi

National Library of Australia
Cataloguing in publication data

Powell, Clifford J.

Spellbound two

Index.

ISBN 0 333 25201 2

1. Spellers.
I. Sadler, Rex Kevin, joint author.
II. Hayllar, Thomas Albert S., joint author.
III. Title.

428'.1

Set in Century by Modgraphic, Adelaide
Printed in Australia at
Griffin Press Limited, Adelaide

Contents

Acknowledgements

The authors and publishers are grateful to the following for permission to reproduce copyright material.

Fibremakers Ltd for p. 68; the Health Commission of New South Wales for p. 106; Hoechst Australia Limited for pp. 1, 125; the *Manly Daily* for pp. 14, 28, 57, 97, 111; the Missionary Aviation Fellowship for p. 47; New Zealand Government Travel Commission for pp. 40, 52, 73; *On Being* magazine (photograph by D. J. McCarthy) for p. 88; Qantas Airways Limited for pp. 19, 36, 83, 121; Victorian Government Department of Sport and Recreation for p. 6; Woolworths for p. 92.

While every care has been taken to trace and acknowledge copyright, the publishers tender their apologies for any accidental infringement where copyright has proved untraceable. They would be pleased to come to a suitable arrangement with the rightful owner in each case.

Preface

Good spelling is no accident. It has to be worked on. The recognition of the one and only grouping of letters that goes to make up a word is no easy skill to acquire. Ideally, words should be taken apart, put back together, looked at in a variety of ways and, above all, *used*. But nobody said this has to be boring!

In the authors' view, there's real learning value in making spelling a pleasure, not a task. *Spellbound Two* (written specially for lower and middle secondary students) presents over 600 everyday words in 30 categories. None of the words is given a chance to lie idly about in lists. They all find themselves pushed around. In puzzles, games and exercises they are dismantled, reconstructed and generally made to work hard. So do the students! But, that's life. Words won't work for you unless you *use* them.

As the key to real motivation is both need and interest, *Spellbound Two*

- puts 600 vitally useful words into the student's and teacher's hands,
- provides ways and means of coming to grips with these words so that interest is kept up and the spell of gaining control over word construction is unbroken.

Well, as spelling is all bound up with words—good spellbinding!

1 FACE TO FACE

sympathy	peculiar
society	successful
welfare	wearily
ordinary	resistance
angrily	curiosity
guilty	intention
loneliness	determined
benefit	deserve
cautious	reputation
ambitious	obstinate

1 How mean are meanings?

Find out by interlocking eight words from the list, using their meanings as clues.

CLUES

1. Feeling sorry for someone
2. When you're absolutely set on doing something
3. For the good of someone or people in general
4. The opinion that others have of you
5. Something you plan or aim to do
6. Stubborn
7. Lacking energy
8. Something that it is good to get

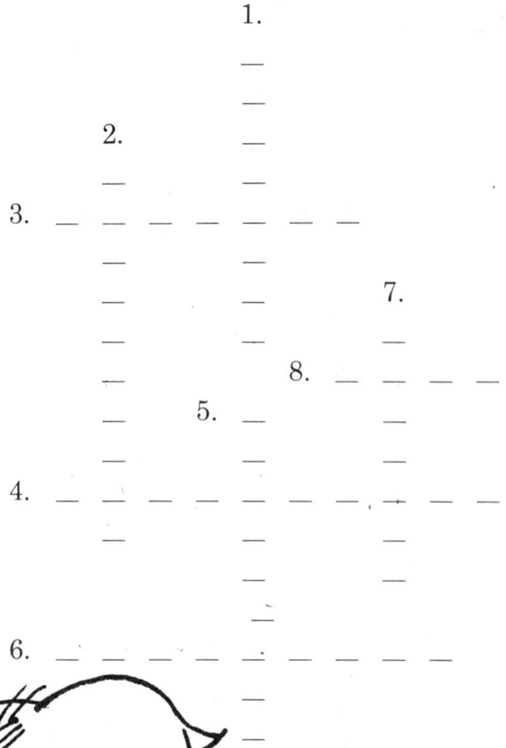

2 Face to face

Read through the following passages, filling in the blanks as you go:

(a) An elderly gentleman was strolling along the street when his .... was aroused by the sight of a small boy standing on tiptoe on the front doorstep of a house and .... reaching up with one hand. As the old gentleman came closer, he saw that the boy's .... was to ring the door bell. Feeling some .... for the boy's obvious difficulty, the elderly gentleman pushed through the front gate and went up to the boy.

'I think you're being a bit too .... Here, allow me.' He rang the bell for the boy and stood back.

'Well, son, now what?'

'I don't know what you're going to do, mister, but I'm going to run like the devil.'

(b) Business was bad at Ronald's Bargain Basement. But, Ronald was no .... businessman. He just wouldn't give up. He was .... to be .... To the right of his Bargain Basement, Basil's Store hung up a .... sign reading: *The greatest going-out-of-business sale ever. You couldn't get a bigger .... from our discounts if we were really going out of business.*

Then Loomies, to the right of Ronald's Bargain Basement, put out their sign. It read: *Fire sale. You .... better buys and you couldn't do better even if there had been a real fire.*

Ronald hung up a sign directly between the other two reading: *Basement entrance to sale.*

3 Opposites

Find list words opposite in meaning to the following words and phrases.

(a) innocent

(b) special

(c) lack of interest

(d) energetically

(e) with no particular desire to achieve great things

(f) rash

(g) callousness

(h) friendship

(i) calmly

4 T time

Form eight list words from the T rectangle. You may use the letters more than once to form your words.

U	F	R	O	B
S	Y	T	A	M
C	E	I	G	N

5 Heads and tails

The words that follow are a mixed-up bunch. Heads have become tails and tails have become heads. Sort them out so that the heads and tails go where they belong.

benety	wearful	obstinion
successily	angary	ordiniety
guilfit	reputated	determinrily
socion	peculity	intentate
curiosiar		

6 Clues

Many list words include other words of three or four letters in their make-up. Using the clues, write down the list word and then underline the word(s) within the words.

(a) The list word surrounds a shelter put up with poles and pegs.

(b) There's one third of a school year in the middle of this word.

(c) A kind of metal is in the middle of this list word.

(d) A list word with a loud noise in the middle.

(e) The end of this list word contains something you pay when you travel.

(f) The end of this list word has something you do in tennis

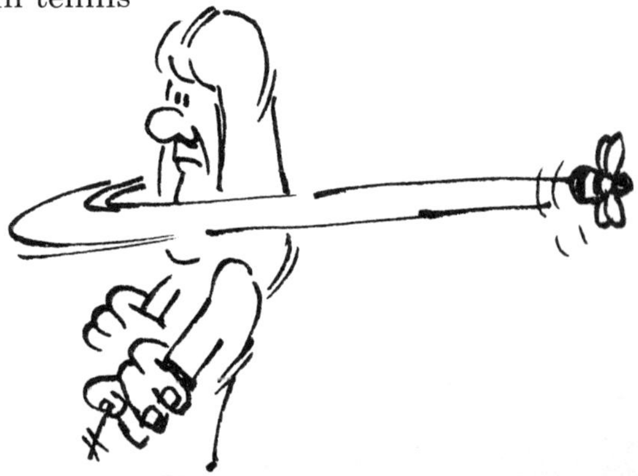

7 Parts of speech

Below is a box of endings. Add them to the basic part of each word to form the part of speech asked for. You should be able to use up all the endings.

ficial	ily	ion	acy	ation	rily
ional	er	e	eed	ious	ity
ion	iness	ately	essfully	ry	
ed	ess	ate	ious	iously	y
fit	ion	ionally	essful		

(a) wear_ _ _ (adverb)
_ _ _ _ _ _(noun)
_ (adjective)

(b) obstin_ _ _ (noun)
_ _ _ (adjective)
_ _ _ _ _ _(adverb)

(c) determin_ _ (past participle)
_ _ _ _ _ _(noun)
_ (verb)

(d) peculiar_ _ _(noun)

(e) succ_ _ _ (verb)
_ _ _ _ _ _ _ _ _ _(adverb)
_ _ _ (noun)
_ _ _ _ _ _ _ (adjective)

(f) ang_ _ (verb)
_ _ _ _ _(adverb)
_ _ (adjective)

(g) bene_ _ _ (verb)
_ _ _ _ _ _ _(adjective)

(h) caut_ _ _ (noun)
_ _ _ _ _ (adjective)
_ _ _ _ _ _ _(adverb)

(i) intent_ _ _ (noun)
_ _ (adverb)
_ _ _ _ _ _ _ _(adjective)

(j) ambit_ _ _ _ _(adjective)
_ _ _ (noun)

2 Life. Be in it.

Larry Lucy Lisa Lenny Lucky

1 Mixed pieces

Make up ten of your list words by joining together the pieces in the box below.

van	cle	ag	lazi	ness	bore
il	cise	spire	dom	ity	al
er	phys	ex	mus	weari	ic
age	ness	per	free	ad	dom

healthy	agility
exercise	physical
strength	advantage
strenuous	perspire
muscle	weariness
fatigue	recreation
effort	laziness
breath	boredom
develop	energetic
bruise	freedom

2 Missing words

Use the correct form of the list word in brackets and insert it in the blank space in each of the following sentences.

(a) .... was running down the face of the runner. [perspire]

(b) He .... threw the ball to his team mates. [energetic]

(c) The swimmer .... swam across the pool. [effortless]

(d) The .... of one's body is helped by physical exercise. [develop]

(e) the cyclist .... pedalled his bike up the hill. [strenuous]

(f) The weightlifter's body was very .... [muscle]

(g) It is important to .... your body by exercising. [strength]

(h) It is .... to exercise daily. [advantage]

(i) She was a very .... tennis player. [agility]

(j) The tennis player was .... superior to the football player. [physical]

3 Fill the blanks

Write down each of the sentences and fill in the blanks by choosing the most appropriate word from the box. (Each word can be used only once.)

agility	freedom	advantage	recreation	perspire
fatigue	exercise	boredom	strenuous	

(a) We tend to .... when we do hard physical exercise.

(b) The runner experienced .... after his .... exercise.

(c) .... generally results from having nothing worthwhile to do.

(d) We often experience a sense of .... in the wide open spaces.

(e) The effective use of .... helps us to enjoy life to the full.

(f) It is an .... to have .... on the squash court.

4 Match the meanings

Put the correct meanings next to each word in the left-hand column.

WORD	MEANING
(a) energetic	relaxation
(b) perspire	nimbleness
(c) recreation	vigorous
(d) fatigue	of the body
(e) physical	sweat
(f) agility	better position or state
(g) freedom	liberty
(h) exercise	tiredness
(i) advantage	exertion of the body

5 Opposites

Write one word that is opposite in meaning to each of the following.

(a) freedom (b) healthy

(c) strength (d) advantage

(e) energetic (f) strenuous

6 Crossword

1. Doing thirty push-ups is ....
2. There was not a .... of wind.
3. After much exercise we experience ....
4. .... people don't get sick very often.
5. (Across) A good athlete must be in fine .... condition.
5. (Down) We all do this in very hot weather.
6. You sometimes receive one of these if you bump into something.
7. A weightlifter has a lot of this.

7 New words

Create new words from your list words by adding an ending from the box.

en	less	al	ly
ment	ally		ous

(a) advantage
(b) develop
(c) physical
(d) energetic
(e) effort
(f) recreation
(g) strengthen

8 Per

The Latin word *per* means 'through' or 'by'. If you receive interest 'per annum', you receive it 'through' or 'by' the year. Fill in the missing letters to complete the words beginning with 'per'. Write their meanings as well.

(a) perc_nt_ge
(b) persp_x
(c) perm_t
(d) perc_late
(e) perm_n_nt
(f) perf_ct
(g) perp_t_al
(h) perf_rate
(i) pers_st
(j) pers_ade

personal	adolescent
amusement	pleasure
handsome	relationship
pretty	concert
romance	favourite
delight	clothes
barbecue	individual
theatre	festival
glamorous	entertainment
affection	celebrity

3 The Trendy Teens

1 Word equations

Solve the following word equations.
(2T+E+PRY=PRETTY)

(a) 2B+CAR+2E=

(b) 2E+2T+AR+H=

(c) 3N+3T+3E+AIM+R=

(d) 2C+NO−IS+TRIES=

(e) SAP+2E+LU+R=

(f) LOAD+2E+TN+CS=

(g) 3I+2D+VAN+LU=

2 Completing the sentences

Using the correct form of the words in brackets, complete the sentences.

(a) It was the .... scene he had ever seen. [pretty]

(b) Many .... were at the pop concert. [celebrity]

(c) The guest speaker made some very .... remarks. [amusement]

(d) The band played a .... tune. [delight]

(e) His .... influenced his actions. [personal]

(f) The bear was .... to the zookeeper. [affection]

(g) The film had one very .... scene. [romance]

(h) The coach tended to .... the best player. [favourite]

3 The E's have it

Build yourself list words by filling round the e's.

(a) _ _ _ _ e _ _ e

(b) _ _ _ _ e _ _

(c) _ e _ _ _ _ _ _

(d) _ _ e _ _ _

(e) _ _ _ _ e _ _ e _ _

(f) e _ _ e _ _ _ _ _ _ e _ _

(g) _ _ e _ _ _ _ e

(h) _ _ e _ _ _ e

(i) _ e _ _ _ _ _ _

(j) _ _ _ _ e _ e _ _

(k) _ e _ e _ _ _ _ _

(l) _ _ _ _ _ _ e

(m) _ e _ _ _ _ _

(n) _ _ _ _ _ _ _ e

(o) _ _ _ e _ _ _ _ _

(p) _ _ _ _ _ _ _ _ e

(q) _ _ _ _ _ e _

(r) _ e _ _ _ _ _ _ _ _ _ _

4 In words

Supply list words to fill the squares by noting the clues to the little 'in' words contained in the list.

1. A word containing a masculine person.
2. This word ends with the opposite of 'dark'.
3. This begins with something that has five fingers on it.
4. Ends with something used in billiards.
5. This word ends with a coin.
6. This one finishes with the idea of two.
7. You can be certain of this one.
8. Ends with a girl's name.
9. It's hot in the middle of this one.
10. This one starts with something blood does.

1. ________
2. ________
3. __________
4. __________
5. _____________
6. _____________
7. __________
8. __________
9. ________
10. ________

5 Party time

Given one word, build around it the other 'party time' words from the list.

6 Word families

Put the right word in its right place in the sentences below. (Note: the words you'll need are supplied in brackets.)

(a) .... is the time of life when pimples are rife. However, an .... can look forward to the disappearance of his or her pimples in time. [adolescent, adolescence]

(b) .... is a lovely state with an increase in heart rate. Most people would agree that modern music is often .... [romantic, romance]

(c) Any .... likes to think that she or he has a distinctive .... [personality, person]

(d) It is a .... to go water-skiing in the summer. Eating can be a .... experience if you're hungry. [delightful, delight]

(e) Spring is a .... time of the year. Many people get .... from leisure. [pleasure, pleasant]

7 Heart throb

See how many list words you can make out of this heart and its throbs. (The central letter R must be used in every word. You may use any of the letters more than once in any word.)

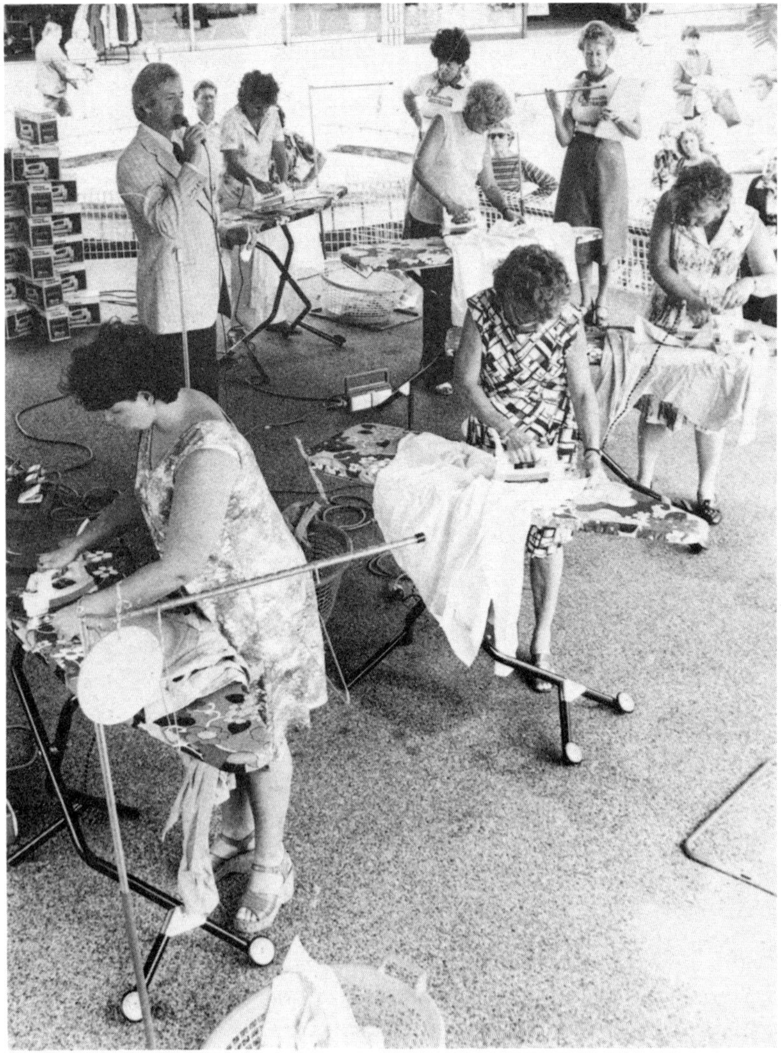

4 Television

channel	documentary
commercial	sponsor
audience	repeat
publicity	national
director	comedy
featuring	special
picture	adventure
popular	producer
episode	screen
survey	variety

1 Star-words

Each of the following star-words contains four list words, with a common letter in the middle. By putting one letter on each space along the lines (starting from the number) and using the letters already provided, find the words that fill out each star. (One word is already filled in.)

```
2       _       3
           _         N    4  _
              _      A    A
                 _   T  _
        1  _  _  _   I  E  _  _  _
                 _   O  _
              _      N    I
           _         A          _
                     L             _
```

```
                                 4
        2  _       3             _
              _    _     _
                V  _  _
1  _  _  _  _   E  _  C  _  _  _
                _  _  _
             T     I     _
        _          _        _
     _             _           _
                                  _
```

2 Word families

Draw up the following table in your workbook. Then build word families for the list words provided, and so fill the blank spaces.

	NOUN	VERB	ADJECTIVE	ADVERB
(a)	publicity			
(b)	director			
(c)			popular	
(d)	producer			
(e)			special	
(f)			commercial	

3 Cryptic clues

Use each clue below to identify its list word.

(a) Has a mixed-up son in its middle.

(b) Starts with a kind of push.

(c) Ends with the initials of National Acoustics Laboratory.

(d) Starts with a common Australian drinking place.

(e) Its end has a mixed up 'very'.

(f) To pass away in its middle.

(g) Ends in jumbled tape.

(h) Starts with Cash On Delivery (initials) in reverse.

(i) A confused dose in the end.

(j) Ends with a confused tenure.

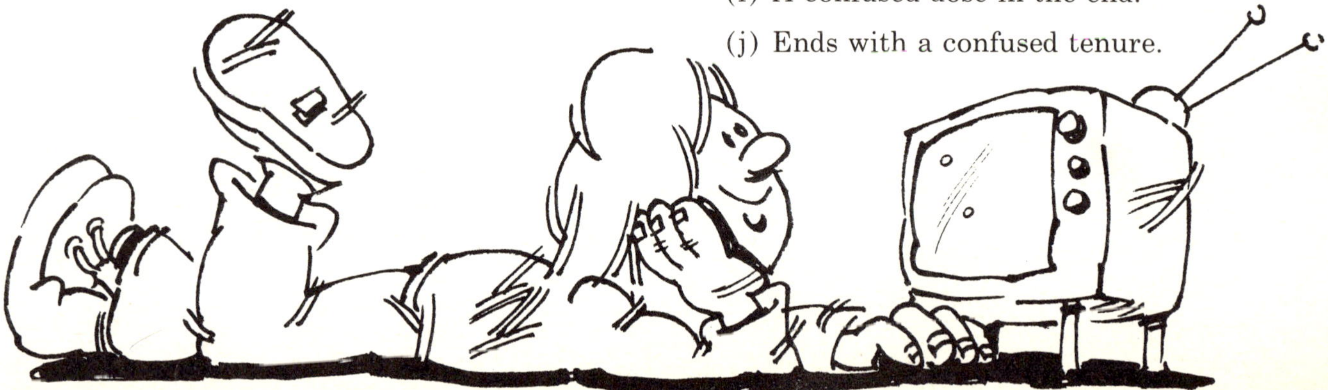

4 Thirds

Every third letter of the following list words is provided. Work out the remaining letters and so identify the words.

(a) __p__a_ (b) __c__e__a__

(c) __i__d_ (d) __r__n

(e) __a__e_ (f) __e__a_

(g) __o__o_ (h) __r__t_

(i) __m__r__a_

5 Two by two

- Divide the class into pairs. Each pair tosses a coin to see which one of the pair goes first.
- The winner of the toss in each case chooses any two words from the list for his partner to spell. Then the partner chooses two words for him to spell, and so on, until the list is covered.
- Scoring: The speller gets one point for every correctly spelt word. His partner gets one point every time the speller makes an error.

6 Mystery word

(a) Use the letters already provided to help you complete the table of list words (one word across each line) below.

(b) Take the letters in the dark squares and rearrange them to discover the mystery list word.

Mystery word: ______________

		M			■					
		O		■						
	■		I	E						
		■	E				R			
			M		■	C				
				M	■			A		

7 Matching definitions

The definitions for each of the list words in the first column are jumbled in their order. Match each list word with its correct definition.

LIST WORD		DEFINITION
(a)	sponsor	a television advertisement
(b)	repeat	the person responsible for all the administration associated with producing a programme
(c)	commercial	a programme that has been shown before on TV
(d)	episode	the company or person who finances a show
(e)	featuring	the person responsible for giving a show its dramatic shape
(f)	director	one night's viewing in a series or a serial
(g)	producer	giving some particular attention to

8 'Or' and 'Er' endings

'Director' ends with 'or' but 'producer' ends with 'er'. Find the naming words for five other people (or things) which end with 'or' and five other people (or things) which end with 'er'. An example of each is provided.

	DIRECTOR	PRODUCER
	tractor	propeller
(a)		
(b)		
(c)		
(d)		
(e)		

5 ABOUT PEOPLE

enthusiasm	apologize
desperate	individual
pleasant	argument
identity	behaviour
conscience	deceive
irritate	courteous
interfere	dissatisfied
innocent	patience
challenge	nuisance
anxiety	routine

1 Word families

Complete the word family table for each of the following list words. (The spelling of two endings has been given to help you.)

	NOUN	VERB	ADJECTIVE	ADVERB
(a)	enthusiasm			...ally
(b)			pleasant	
(c)		deceive		
(d)		apologize		...ally
(e)		irritate		
(f)		interfere		

2 Criss-cross words

Six list words (across and down) are contained in the criss-cross below. Use the clues to find each word.

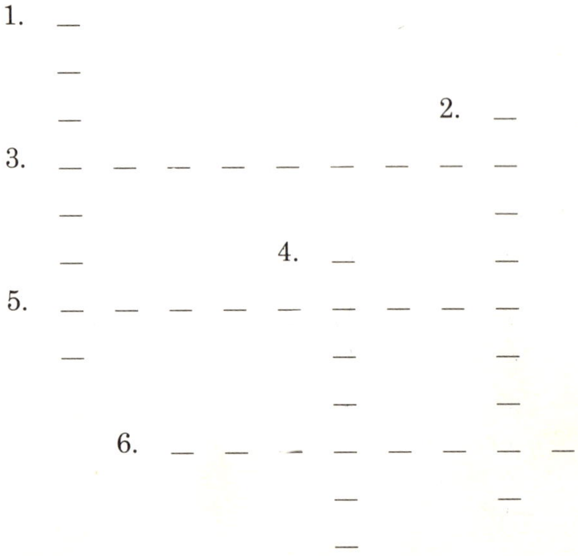

CLUES
1. Long-suffering
2. Willing to try anything
3. Meddle
4. Mislead
5. Invite to a contest
6. Annoy

3 Word wheels

Each word wheel below contains two list words. Experiment to find your starting letter for each word, and then find the rest of the word by taking every *second* letter, moving clockwise.

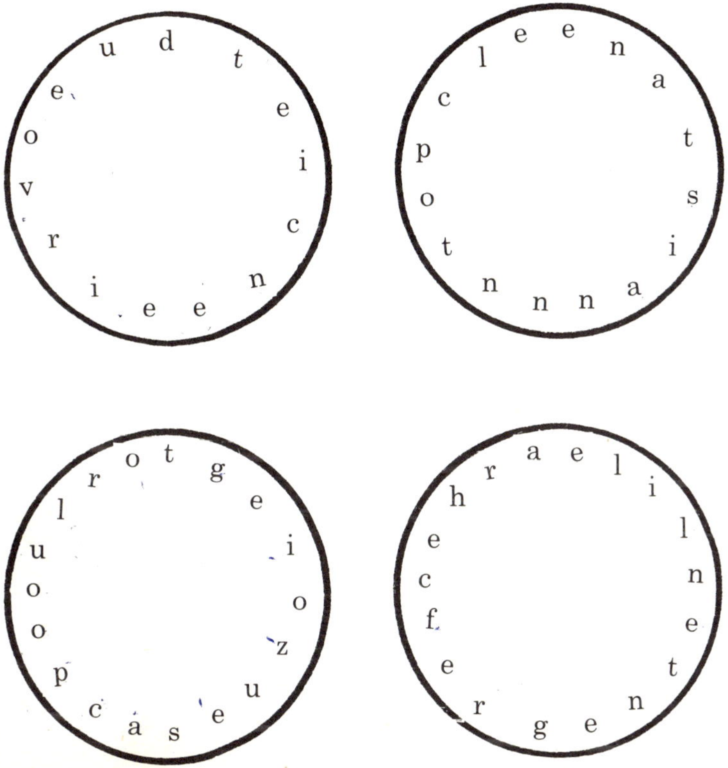

4 Cryptic clues

Use the clues to identify words from the list.

(a) Out shortly after the start.

(b) Has a confused fist just after its middle.

(c) In no decimal currency.

(d) A chewy tree in the middle.

(e) Starts where you play tennis.

(f) A lump of wood in its middle.

(g) Confused Illinois Test of Psycholinguistic Abilities (initials) to start with.

(h) Takes most of a dive in its middle.

(i) Needs a panel-beater shortly after its start.

(j) Yet ends confused.

5 Antonyms (Opposites)

(a) Find antonyms for each of the following list words by adding a prefix.
 pleasant, courteous, patience

(b) Find list words which are antonyms to the following words.
 variety, indifference, satisfied, guilty, offend, group

6 Mystery word

(a) Use the letters already provided to complete one list word along each line of the table below.

(b) Take the letters in the dark squares and rearrange them to find the mystery list word.

Mystery word: _ _ _ _ _ _ _ _ _ _

■	N			E					
		C				■			
	■	I				C			
		N			E		■		
			L		■			E	
	O		■			O			
		T					A		■
		■			I			C	

7 Clichés

A cliché is a group of words that has been used so often that it has lost all freshness and force, e.g. 'millions of times'. Use list words to complete these clichés.

(a) a clear ....

(b) a .... situation

(c) a .... walk

(d) with wild ....

(e) with never-ending ....

(f) the same old ....

(g) be on your best ....

6 Keeping in Touch

address	congratulations
signature	receive
initial	faithfully
paragraph	telephone
typewriter	punctuation
language	sincerely
postage	envelope
correspondence	information
complaint	delivery
written	registered

1 Letter rip

Look at the letter outline below, then answer the questions indicated by the arrows.

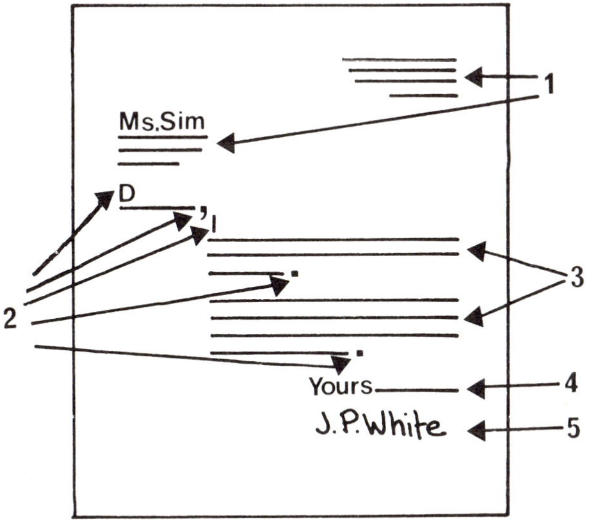

1. Which list word is appropriate for both '1's?
2. Which list word describes all the features indicated by these arrows?
3. Each of these 'blocks' of writing is called a ....
4. Two list words would be equally suitable here. What are they?
5. An 8-letter form of a list word describes these letters that belong to White, the letter writer.

2 Taking a licking

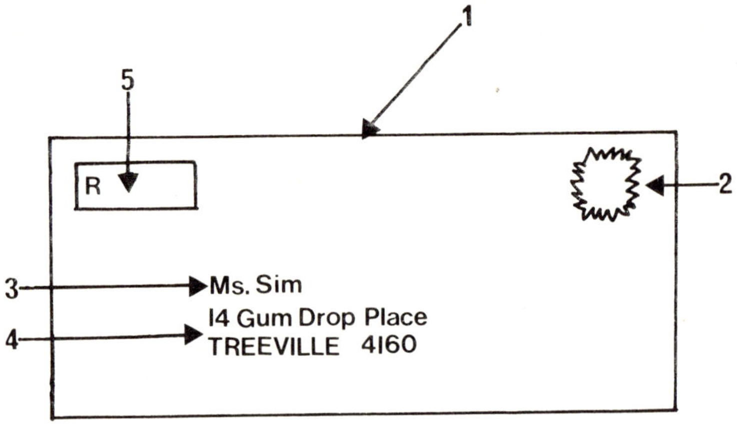

(a) This object is, of course, an ....

(b) Here's the expected .... stamp.

(c) Ms Sim, the person to whom the letter is written, is also known as the ....ee. [Place a list word in the space in front of the 'ee'.]

(d) All this can be hand .... or produced by a ....

(e) The Post Office places a sticker on the ....e if the letter is sent by ....d mail. This is a method of ....y that guarantees the safety of a letter.

3 Centre word

List words about letter writing will fit the squares below. The first step is to find the Centre Word (1 down). Then go on to find the across words. Clues below.

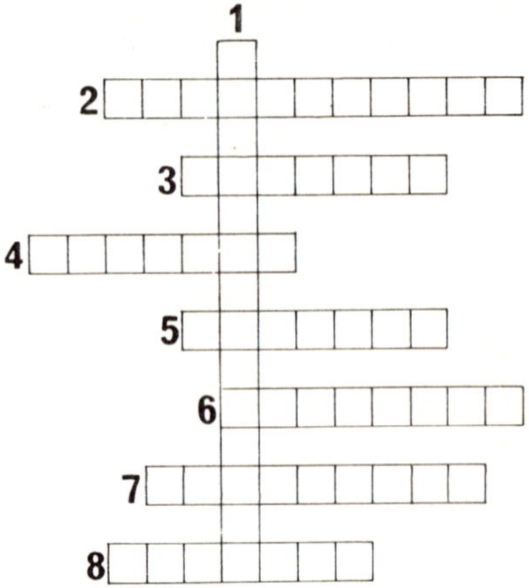

CLUES

1 Down: A number of letters written about a certain topic
2 Across: Details about a certain topic
3 Across: Put down on paper
4 Across: This makes sure the letter reaches its destination
5 Across: The payment you make to have your letter sent
6 Across: The letter arrives
7 Across: Yours ....
8 Across: To have the letter in hand

4 ····/·/·—··/·—··/———// —/····/·/·—·/·//

If you don't like letter writing, another method of communication is *Morse code*. In this code, combinations of dots and dashes are used to represent the letters of the alphabet.

What message is contained in the heading to this exercise?

A	·—	N	—·
B	—···	O	———
C	—·—·	P	·——·
D	—··	Q	——·—
E	·	R	·—·
F	··—·	S	···
G	——·	T	—
H	····	U	··—
I	··	V	···—
J	·———	W	·——
K	—·—	X	—··—
L	·—··	Y	—·——
M	——	Z	——··

5 ——/·/···/···/·—/——·/·//

Work out this message in Morse and put yourself in touch with *five* list words as you go.

NOTE: Each letter is separated from the next by one sloping line, while each word is separated by a double sloping line.

—·—·/———/—·/——·/·—·/·—/—/··—/·—··/
·—/—/··/———/—·/···//—·——/———/··—//
····/·—/···—/·//·———/··—/···/—//
···/———/·—··/···—/·/—··//—/····/·//
··—·/··/·—·/···/—//·——/———/·—·/—··//
—·/———/·——//—/·—·/—·——//—/····/·/
···/·//·—·/·/—·—·/·/··/···—/·//·——/·—·/··/
—/—/·/—·//·—/—··/—··/·—·/·/···/···//—··/·/
·—··/··/···—/·/·—·/—·——//

6 Open lines

The open lines span quite a few list words and give you a letter in each. Discover the words in full.

(a) _ _ _ _ _ _ _ _ E

(b) _ _ _ _ _ _ _ L _ _

(c) _ _ _ _ _ _ E

(d) _ _ _ _ _ R _ _ _ _

(e) _ _ _ _ T _ _ _ _ _ _

(f) _ _ _ P _ _ _ _ _

(g) _ _ N _ _ _ _ _

(h) _ Y _ _ _ _ _ _ _ _

(i) C _ _ _ _ _ _ _ _ _ _ _ _ _

7 You're connected

Key list words in the following phone-ins have their letters scrambled. Unscramble them to find out exactly what the operator is saying.

At the third pip you
will everiec a time
check.

This is your friendly
notephole operator. Go
ahead, please.

This is directory
otninriofam. Please
go ahead . . .

You have lost your coins?
Kindly give me your name
and sedrasd and the money
will be refunded.

You wish to send a
sutonatnargiocl telegram?
Please go ahead . . .

Yes, madam, your mclotniap has
been noted and will be looked
into.

You will be sent a directory if you forward
us $1.00 for tepgaso. Now, what
are your sitlaini, Mr Ford?

Watch your neglaaug, please!

8 Stamp your letters

In each of the 'stamps' below there is a central letter surrounded by other letters. Form list words from the letters given, being sure to include the central letter in each word. You may use letters more than once.

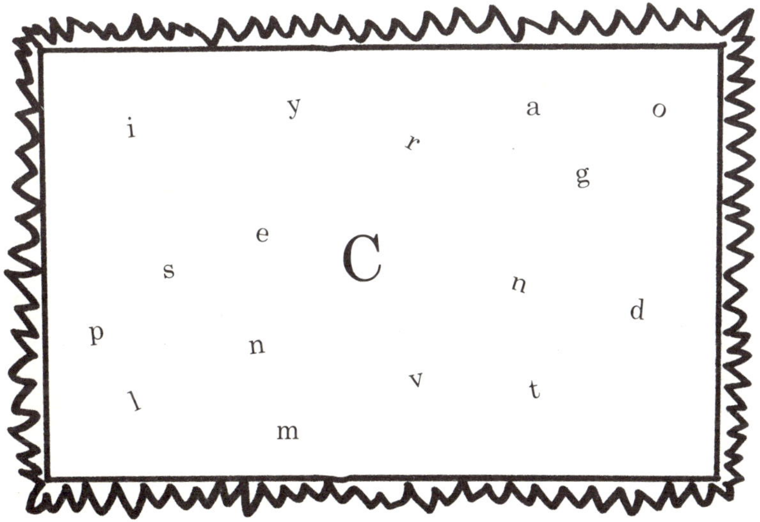

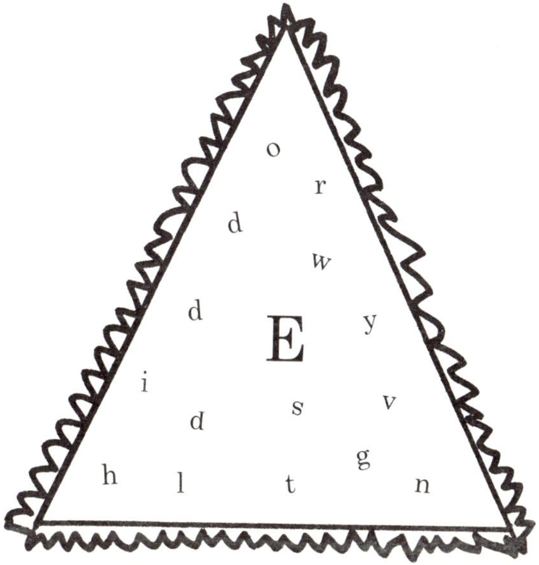

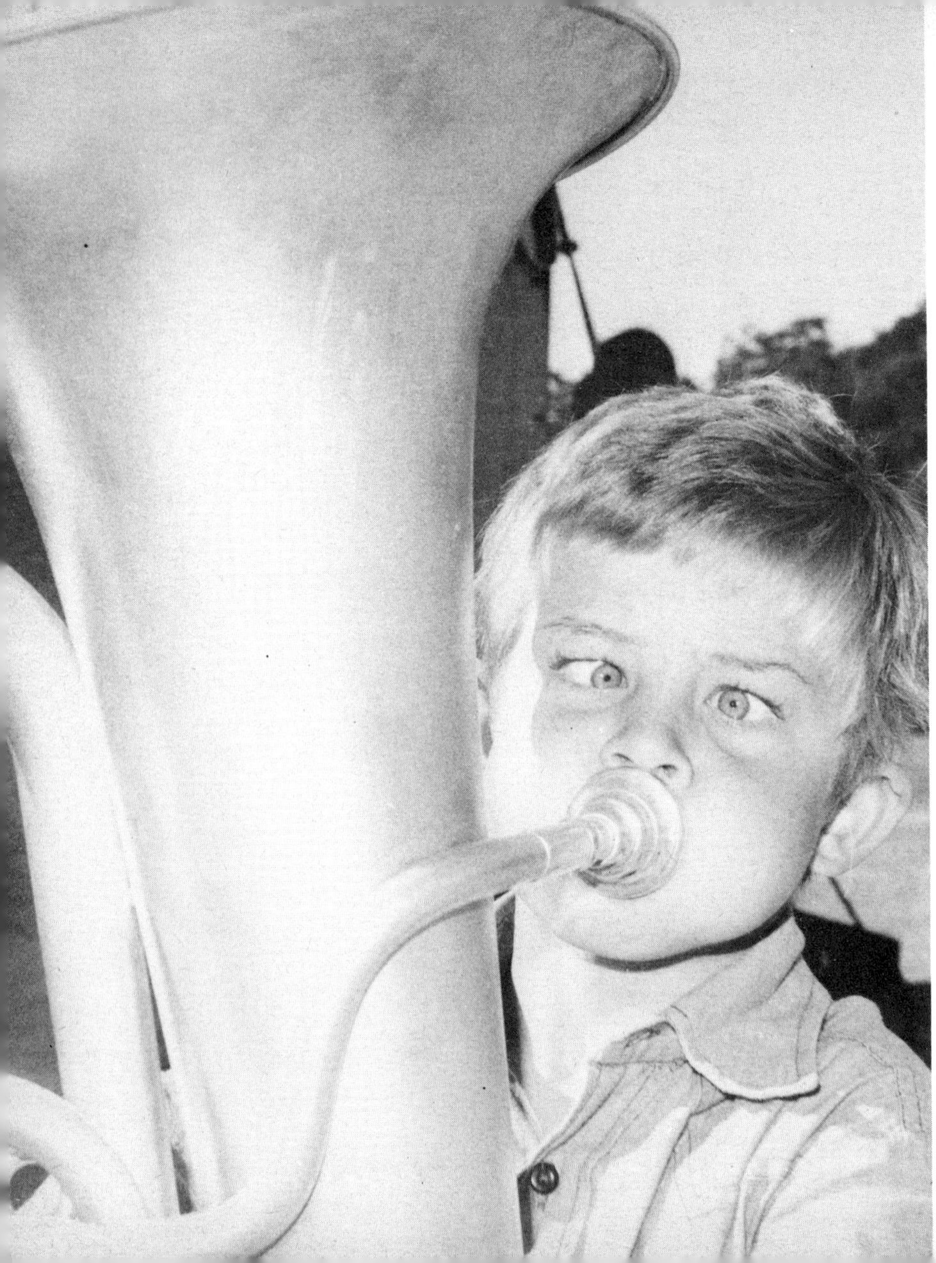

7 SPELLBINDER ONE

preserve	unique
provide	contribute
protection	spectacular
possess	preference
precede	treasure
obtain	confidence
accomplish	reliable
acquire	affection
acceptance	sufficient
mischievous	plentiful

1 Missing words

Use the correct forms of list words in the brackets to complete the sentences.

(a) Sometimes parents can be over............ . [protection]

(b) The headmistress established a .... when she allowed students to come to school in jeans. [precede]

(c) The new student was involved in a great deal of .... [mischievous]

(d) He makes a weekly .... to Medibank. [contribute]

(e) The student's behaviour was not .... to the new teacher. [acceptance]

(f) Very often teachers .... on the co-operation of their students. [reliable]

(g) The headmaster .... to abandon the excursion. [preference]

(h) The class had .... many positive results in the biology experiments. [obtain]

(i) It is important that we be concerned about the .... of our wild life. [preserve]

2 Clues

Use these clues to help you identify words from your list.

(a) The first three letters of this list word are an abbreviation of 'university'.

(b) The middle three letters of this word are an important part of the chest. Eve is said to have been made from one.

(c) In the middle of this word you'll find 'cat' spelled backwards.

(d) The ending of this word is something important you do when you play tennis.

(e) This word has the past tense of 'loan' in it.

(f) The last four letters of this word are very certain.

(g) The last five letters of this word have the same sound as in 'choir'.

(h) These two list words begin with the name given to most golf teachers.

(i) You'll find the abbreviation for 'referee' in this word.

(j) This word has the abbreviation for 'competition' in it.

3 Meanings

Find the list word that is closest in meaning to each of the following definitions.

(a) precious gems or metals

(b) to keep the same quality

(c) to give

(d) more than sufficient

(e) naughty

(f) favouring

4 Word building

Fill in the blanks to form new words.

(a) preserve	preserv_t__n, preserv_t_ve, preserv__g.
(b) accomplish	accomplishm_n_, accomplish_d, accomplish_n_.
(c) protection	protect_v_, protect_r, protect_.
(d) confidence	confiden_, confident_y.
(e) preference	prefer__d, preferent__l, prefer__le, preferr__g.

5 Match the meanings

Write down the left-hand column. Then next to each word write its meaning from the second column.

(a) precede	enough
(b) protective	love
(c) affection	having no equal
(d) reliable	go before
(e) sufficient	supply
(f) provide	defence
(g) accomplish	gain
(h) possess	dependable
(i) unique	to own
(j) acquire	complete

6 Spellbinder salad

Find the following twelve list words in the salad.

provide	preference	plentiful
treasure	possess	acquire
protection	preserve	accomplish
reliable	unique	obtain

D	E	C	N	E	R	E	F	E	R	P
N	O	I	T	C	E	T	O	R	P	R
F	H	L	E	N	I	A	T	B	O	O
E	E	V	R	E	S	E	R	P	S	V
L	U	F	I	T	N	E	L	P	S	I
S	E	R	U	S	A	E	R	T	E	D
U	N	I	Q	U	E	E	R	S	S	E
M	A	C	C	O	M	P	L	I	S	H
E	L	B	A	I	L	E	R	C	O	V

7 Where words come from

The Latin word *pre* means before. Work out the following words that begin with *pre* and write down their meanings.

(a) pred___t	tell beforehand
(b) prefabr_c_te	make before
(c) pref___e	the part of the book which comes first
(d) prem_t_re	before the proper time
(e) premed_t_te	think out beforehand
(f) pre_ud_e	pass judgement before trial

8 Mis-

'Mis' at the beginning of a word means 'not'. Below are ten words. 'Mis' can be added to only five of these. Find the five words and add 'mis' to them.

govern	envelope
distance	judge
calculate	interest
impatience	lay
fortune	attentive

8 LEARNING TO DRIVE

safety	reverse
maintenance	permission
pedestrian	provisional
vehicle	intersection
collision	licence
mechanical	anticipate
automatic	pressure
instructor	situation
accelerate	requires
accident	negligent

1 Got the clues?

Find a word from the list above to fit each of the following clues.

(a) An important piece of paper for a driver

(b) Something you check about your tyres

(c) This term could apply to a horse and cart or a semi-trailer.

(d) A nerve-racking occupation?

(e) The place where roads meet

(f) The noun from 'collide'

(g) You don't have to bother changing gears in this car.

(h) Regular .... can help avoid unexpected engine failure.

(i) What you are if you don't concentrate while you drive

(j) Important that you do this to pass another car

2 Missing letters

Every third letter of the following list words is provided. Find the missing letters and work out the words.

(a) __c__e__
(b) __t__i__t_
(c) __d__t__a_
(d) __r__s__o_
(e) __o__s__n__
(f) __q__r__
(g) __v__s_
(h) __f__y
(i) __h__l_
(j) __c__n__a_

3 Completing

Use the correct form of each of the list words to complete the following sentences.

(a) He pressed the .... to the floor. [accelerate]

(b) The taxi .... with a small utility loaded with bottles. [collision]

(c) The young driver showed great .... in avoiding the animal. [anticipate]

(d) Reverse parking was the only .... he failed. [requires]

(e) Though it looked old, the bike was .... sound. [mechanical]

(f) Time spent in .... a car is usually well worth while. [maintenance]

(g) The team navigator gave .... on which roads to follow. [instructor]

(h) He picked up his learner's .... the day he was eligible. [permission]

4 Mix and match

Match the beginnings from the second column with their correct endings from the first column, and find the list words.

	ENDING	BEGINNING
(a)	gent	li
(b)	cence	acc
(c)	ision	mainten
(d)	sure	negli
(e)	elerate	pres
(f)	ical	pro
(g)	verse	coll
(h)	ident	acc
(i)	ance	mechan
(j)	visional	re

5 Word wheels

Each group of letters on the car contains two list words. Find the correct starting letter, then take every *second* letter (moving clockwise) in order to find the words.

6 Missing

Fill in the missing letters to find the list words.

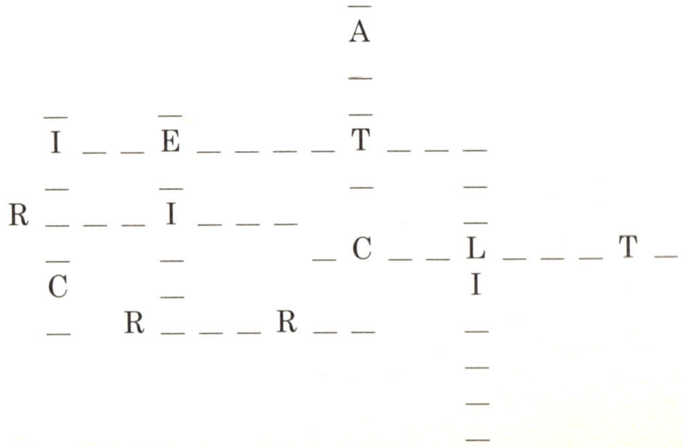

7 Word families

Fill in the blanks in the word family table below.

	NOUN	ADJECTIVE	ADVERB
(a)	safety	....	....
(b)	accident	....	....
(c)	....	automatic	....
(d)	....	negligent	....
(e)	....	provisional	....
(f)	permission	....	....

8 Spell-a-word (variation)

1. Divide the class into two teams. Then a person in Team One asks a person in Team Two to spell a word from one of the spelling lists studied.
2. If the person in Team Two gets it right, Team Two gets a point, which is noted on the blackboard. If the person in Team Two cannot spell the word, Team One gets a point. Whatever happens, the person in Team Two who has just spelled the word, now asks a different person in Team One to spell another word.
3. Total the points earned by each team to find the winner. Scores can be kept on the blackboard.

9 Guess Who's Coming to Dinner?

delicious	stomach
biscuit	picnic
thirsty	recipe
digestion	magnificent
hungrily	enjoyable
flavour	poultry
nutritious	juice
luncheon	groceries
appreciate	alcohol
calorie	chocolate

1 Clues

Use the clues to find the list words.

(a) This word ends with the plural of 'me'.

(b) The ending of this word is something pigs live in.

(c) This word ends with something to keep you cool.

(d) This word rhymes with a little word that means to 'put effort in'.

(e) If you turn the middle of this word back to front you have part of a fish.

(f) This word begins with a word that is slang for 'mad' or 'stupid'.

(g) The second and third letters of this word form the singular of 'are'.

(h) The end of this word is an abbreviation that means 'that is'.

(i) The first three letters of this word describe what miners do.

(j) The last part of this word means 'not on time'.

2 Completing

Look at the word in brackets at the end of each sentence. Then use the correct form of this word in the sentence.

(a) The explorer .... drank the water. [thirsty]

(b) The .... system of the rat was being studied by the scientists. [digestion]

(c) His .... caused him to eat greedily. [hungrily]

(d) The crowd showed their .... by clapping loudly. [appreciate]

(e) The boy was eating a large .... peach. [juice]

(f) The punch that the hostess had prepared was .... [alcohol]

(g) The celebrity received much .... working for charity. [enjoyable]

(h) He decided to reduce his intake of .... [calorie]

3 Nouns

Change to nouns.

(a) appreciate (b) enjoyable (c) hungrily

(d) magnificent (e) nutritious (f) thirsty

4 Scrambled letters

Unscramble the letters to form list words.

(a) h c e a o t l o

(b) i l e r a o c

(c) b y e e o n a l j

(d) s i t u r u i t n o

(e) l o y r p t u

(f) c o a t s h m

(g) e e c i p r

5 Match the meanings

(a) recipe	nourishing
(b) delicious	to be aware of the value of something
(c) nutritious	fowls
(d) appreciate	explanation and list of ingredients for preparing a meal
(e) calorie	excellent
(f) juice	very tasty
(g) poultry	made from cacao-seed
(h) chocolate	unit of amount of food or heat
(i) magnificent	special taste
(j) flavour	liquid, especially from fruit or vegetable

6 Selecting words

Select the most appropriate words from the box and place them in the spaces provided.

stomach	luncheon
thirsty	groceries
chocolate	appreciate
recipe	delicious

(a) The hot .... was .... to drink.

(b) The politician spoke at the ....

(c) The biscuits made from the new .... were enjoyable.

(d) At the picnic the .... dog drank the water.

(e) The teacher will .... the gift of ....

(f) The guest had a .... upset.

7 Crossword without the usual clues

Work out the crossword, using as your clues the three letters given. You will need nine list words.

10 DANGER, DANGER, DANGER

wreckage	suffocate
threaten	collapse
frightened	vicious
suffering	hostage
casualty	destruction
survive	explosion
tragedy	victim
emergency	attack
injury	disaster
rescue	violence

1 IOs and SUs

These two letter combinations can be found in some of the list words. With the IOs and the SUs in place, complete the patterns.

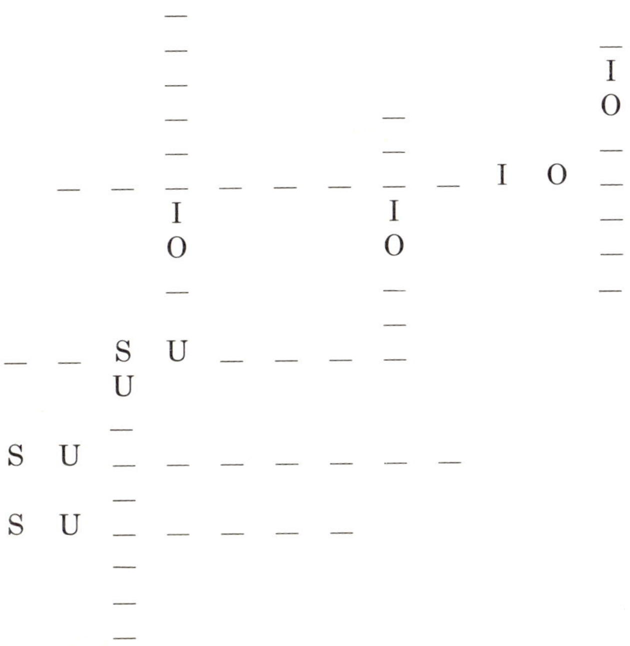

2 Wild weather

Find list words that will fit correctly into the blanks in the following report on some wild, wild weather. To help you, the number of letters for each word is shown, and sometimes the first letter is given.

The cyclone hit the coast with v_ _ _ _ _ _ force. The v_ _ l_ _ _ _ of the wind and rain seemed to _ _ _ _ _ _ _ _ _ the town that stood in its path with total _ _ _ _ _ _ _ _ _ _ _ _.

This natural _ _ _ _ _ _ _ _ _ caused _ _ _ _ _ _ _ _ _ _ _ residents to seek the shelter of the strongest rooms of their houses that could withstand the possible _ _ _ _ _ _ _ _ _ _ of roofs.

A state of _ _ _ _ _ _ _ _ _ _ was declared with the simple aim of helping everybody to s_ _ _ _ _ _ the cyclone. The _ _ _ _ _ _ _ _ _ section of the hospital was put on standby alert to deal with any _ _ _ _ _ _ _.

When the storm finally roared back out to sea, a full-scale _ _ _ _ _ _ _ operation was undertaken. Its purpose was to locate every _ _ _ _ _ _ _ of the _ _ _ _ _ _ _ _ and also to alleviate the s_ _ _ _ _ _ _ _ _ of those who had been made homeless.

3 Exploding words

Words have exploded below. However, the bits in the air can be joined with the pieces on the ground to form list words—with a difference. There's the noun and the verb form of each list word. Place each form in the appropriate column below. (Leading letters are given.)

NOTE: You'll find a few of the words on the ground do not need any of the bits in the air to form *their* nouns or verbs.

NOUNS	VERBS
S	S
W	W
T	T
S	S
I	I
D	D
E	E
S	S

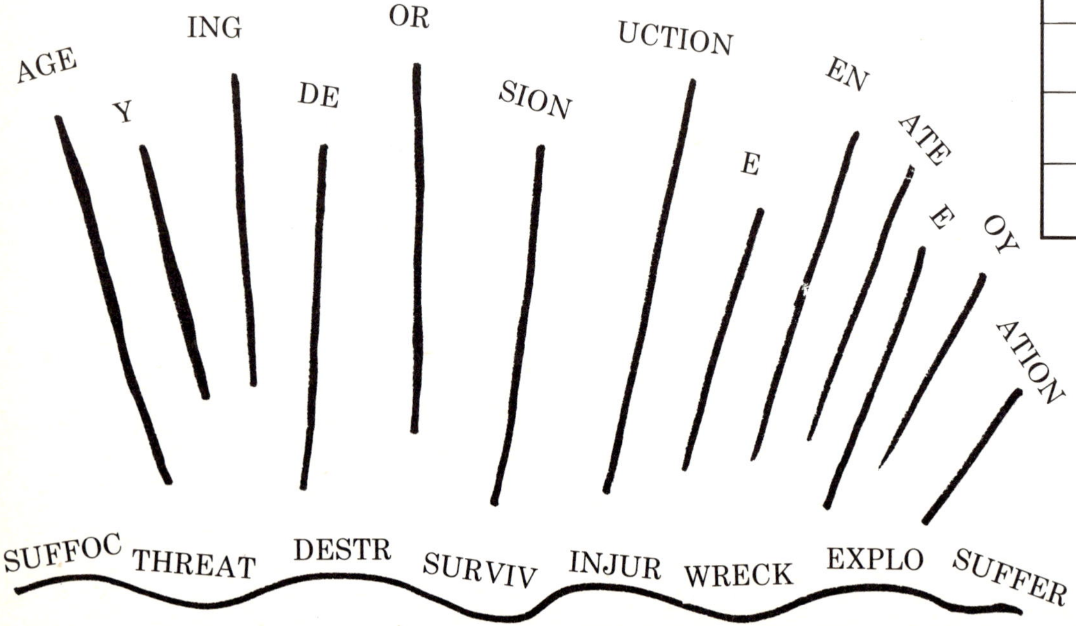

4 ATEs, AGEs and Ys

Find the list words using these clues:

(a) the ATE that lacks air
(b) the AGE that is no longer any use
(c) the Y that is a crisis
(d) the AGE without freedom
(e) the Y that is a hospital department
(f) the Y that has suffered an accident
(g) the Y that is a terrible happening

5 Win in

Which word is the winner? Well, it's going to be the word that supplies you with the most words within words. One little word is given for each of the three to start you off:

FRIGHTENED	DESTRUCTION	SUFFOCATE
ten	tin	fate

6 Hidden words

Rearrange the letters in the two diagrams to discover twelve list words. Use the brief clues to help you.

Nothing gentle	O	E	C	E	I	N	L	V			
The big bang	I	O	L	S	X	O	E	N	P		
Pulling down	T	N	R	S	T	I	O	E	D	C	U
Scared	R	N	E	D	G	E	T	I	H	F	
Feeling pain	F	N	I	R	S	G	E	F	U		
A crisis	E	Y	G	N	E	C	E	R	M		

Lack breath	O	E	C	U	A	T	F	S	F
Captive	S	E	A	H	G	T	O		
Terrible event	T	I	R	D	S	E	S	A	
Menace	T	N	E	E	A	T	R	H	
Unable to stand	P	A	S	O	L	E	L	C	
In pieces	C	A	K	G	W	E	E	R	

When the unscrambled list words are fitted into these two diagrams, two more hidden words can be found. Follow the Xs from top to bottom.

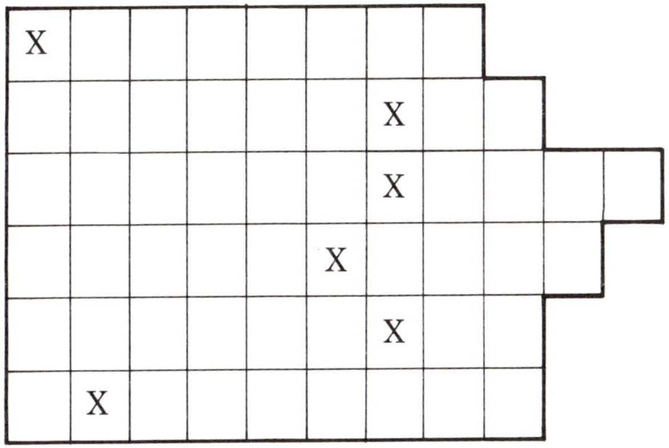

B

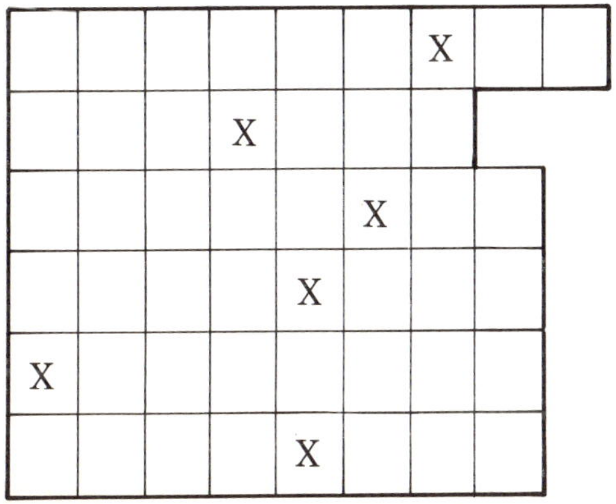

7 Complete collapse

The 'complete collapse' below is pinning down nine list words. See if you can rescue them by proceeding letter by letter, starting at S and going up, down, left or right, but *not* diagonally.
Example:

R
S—U Get the idea? Off you rush!

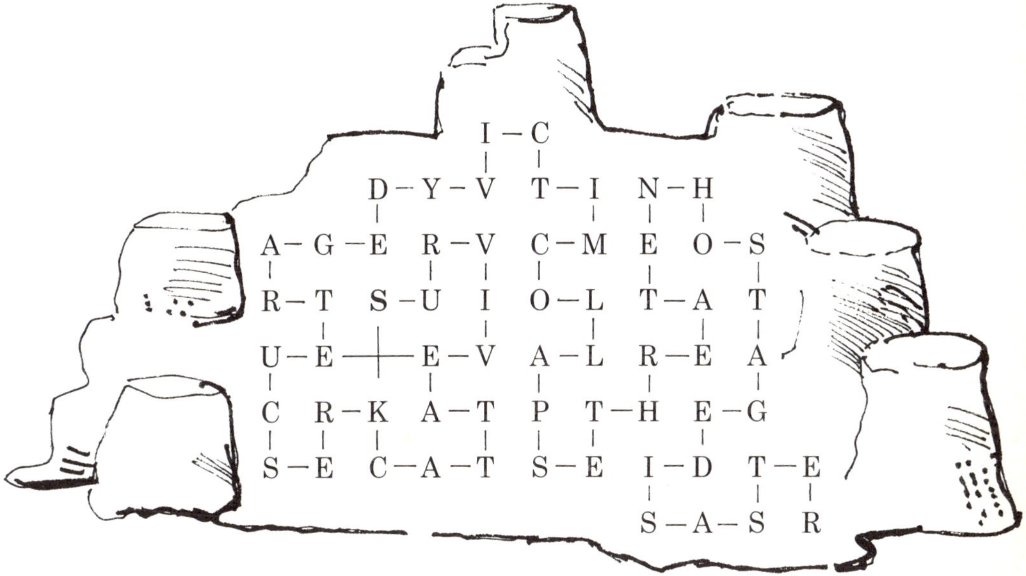

8 Double trouble

Work out the list words by filling in the missing letters.

(a) _i__i_

(b) __ll____

(c) t____t__

(d) _e___e

(e) ___v_v_

(f) __ff_____

(g) _tt___

(h) __s_s___

(i) __ff_____

(j) _i_i___

(k) _a__a___

(l) ___t___t___

(m) ____o__o_

11 SPELLBINDER TWO

delicate	official
noticeable	peculiar
considerate	critical
increase	inferior
prejudice	ridiculous
necessary	embarrass
permanent	research
precise	convey
technique	marriage
original	progress

1 Use the clues!

Use each of the following clues to identify a word from the list.

(a) Alcoholic drink in the middle.

(b) Lucid backwards in the middle.

(c) Ends with a jumbled italic.

(d) A backwards male sheep to begin with.

(e) Does not tell the truth at the end.

(f) Jumbled 'ream' and 'brass'.

(g) Confused name in the middle.

(h) More than one die to finish.

(i) Ends with an arch.

(j) Ends with ease.

2 Criss-cross word

Eight list words are contained in the criss-cross below. Use the letters already given as a guide, and so identify the words.

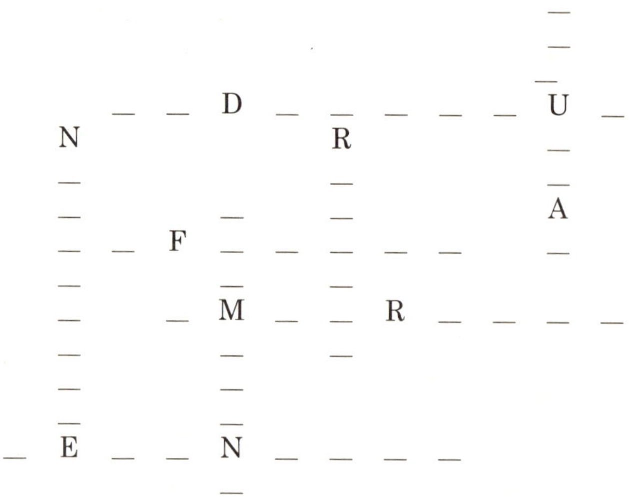

3 Mystery word

(a) Use the letters already provided to help you fill in the blanks below, and so identify one list word for each line across the table.

(b) Take the letters in the dark squares and rearrange them to find the mystery list word.

				E	■				
	■		C						
		■	U						
	F			C		■			
			G		■				
	R				E		■		
	■		H					E	
		B				A	■		
				C	■			L	

4 Using the correct form of the word

Use the correct form of each list word in brackets to complete the following sentences.

(a) The gymnastics squad went through their routine with the .... of a professional group. [precise]

(b) For one .... moment the two girls stared at each other's dress. [embarrass]

(c) For a small .... the parking attendant found a spot right near the ticket office. [considerate]

(d) There was a noticeable .... in the golfer's swing. [peculiar]

(e) Sweeping .... finally destroyed the relationship of trust between the two partners. [critical]

(f) The .... for physical fitness led to the jogging program. [necessary]

(g) Many patrons considered the snails to be the restaurant's outstanding .... [delicate]

(h) The attempt to .... the committee's findings proved a failure. [ridiculous]

5 Star-words

Each of the following star-words contains four list words with a common letter in the middle. By using one letter for each space along the lines (starting from the number each time), and using the letters already provided, find the words that fill out each star. One word in the first star is already filled in for you.

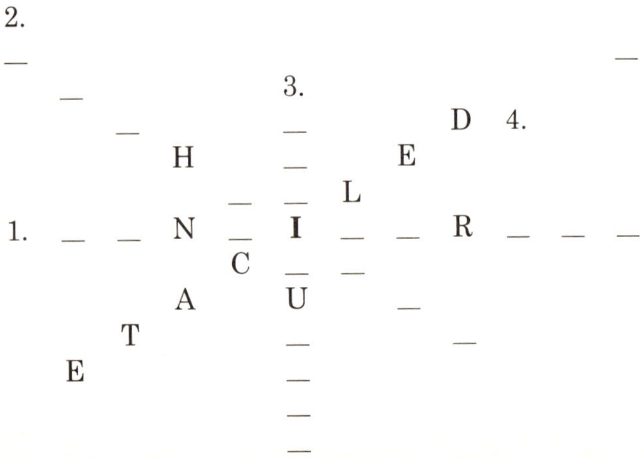

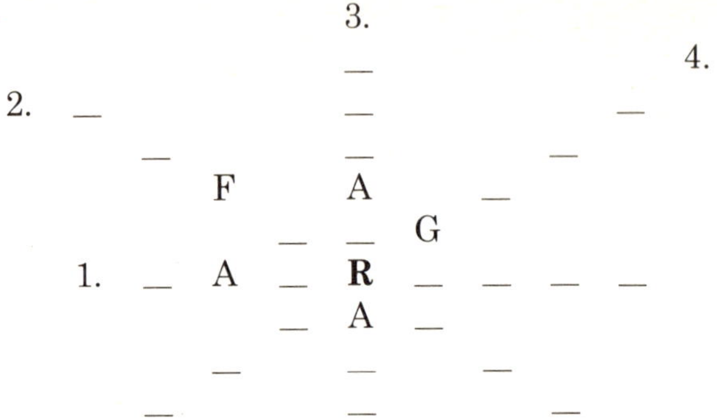

6 Antonyms (Opposites)

(a) By adding a prefix to each of the following list words, form their antonyms.

necessary	original
critical	official
noticeable	precise
considerate	

(b) Find the correct antonyms for each of the following list words from the antonym list.

LIST WORD	ANTONYM
delicate	regress
increase	superior
inferior	divorce
progress	decrease
marriage	strong

7 Word wheels

Each word wheel below contains two list words. Experiment to find your starting letter for each word, then find the rest of the word by taking every *second* letter, moving clockwise.

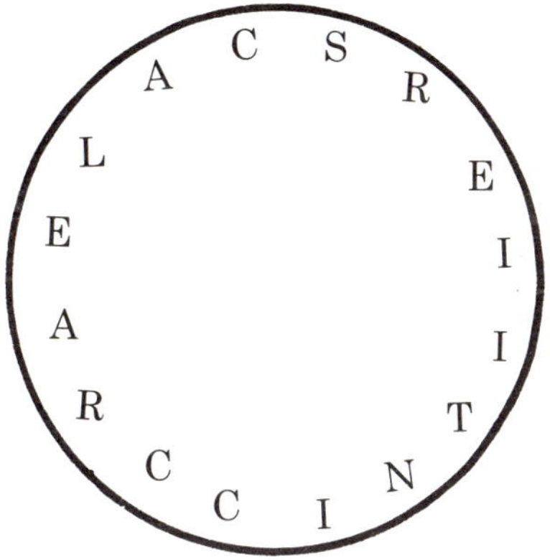

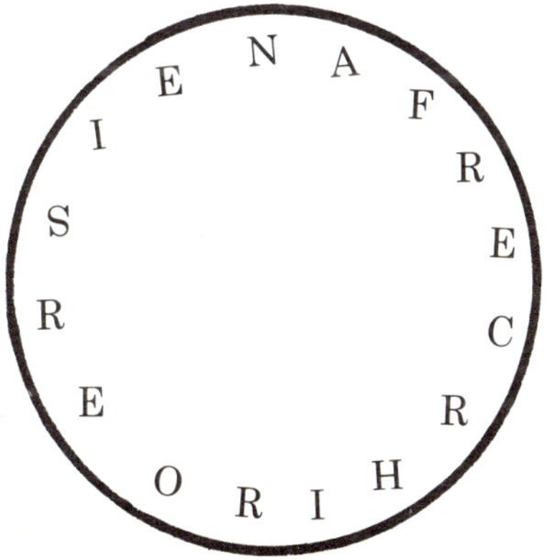

12 GOING PLACES

foreign	marvellous
tourist	luggage
guide	accommodation
holiday	discount
vacation	diary
traveller	relaxation
pamphlet	destination
scenery	choice
souvenir	expense
cruise	convenient

1 Use the clues!

Find a word from the list above to fit each of the following clues.

(a) Has a jumbled level in it.

(b) Its middle would chase a mouse.

(c) Begins with a backwards map.

(d) Begins with a backwards raid.

(e) Ends with a cold substance.

(f) Has a writing implement in its middle.

(g) Has a backwards tax in its middle.

(h) Ends with a king's rule.

(i) Has a metal in its middle.

(j) Ends with someone like a duke.

2 Synonyms

Column 1 contains a group of jumbled synonyms for the list words in Column 2. Match each synonym with its correct list word.

	SYNONYMS	LIST WORDS
(a)	strange	pamphlet
(b)	sightseer	scenery
(c)	brochure	relaxation
(d)	views	cruise
(e)	wonderful	foreign
(f)	lodgings	marvellous
(g)	resting	tourist
(h)	boat-trip	accommodation

3 Word wheels

Each word wheel contains two list words. Once you find the first letter of each word, you work the word out by taking every *second* letter, moving clockwise.

4 Design a travel poster or advertisement

Design your own eye-catching travel poster or advertisement using as many list words as you can. Here's an example, but you'll be able to do much better. Display your efforts in the class.

5 Missing words

Use the correct form of the list words to complete each of the following sentences.

(a) The motel proved to be .... [expense]

(b) The particular room we had was able to .... a family of six. [accommodation]

(c) We spent a most .... week there. [relaxation]

(d) The .... of being waited on meant that the expense was worthwhile. [convenient]

(e) .... views were within walking distance. [scenery]

(f) When we left we purchased a .... teaspoon to remind us of the holiday. [souvenir]

6 Mystery word

(a) Each line across in the table below is a list word. Use the letters given as clues to help you find the words.

(b) Take the letters in the dark squares and re-arrange them to find the mystery list word.

Mystery word: ________________

	U	■	D							
	R	■			E					
		P		N	■					
S	■					I				
■	R		V							
■		L				T				
	E			I			■			N

7 Jumbled words

Re-arrange the following letters to form list words.

(a) iosrvune (b) ndacmtamooico

(c) alohdyi (d) txerinoala

(e) ysrence (f) osntiduc

8 Symbols

List words are symbolized in the diagrams below.
Identify each list word.

approximately	surely
truly	naturally
eventually	generally
particularly	considerably
probably	economically
equally	nearly
regularly	fiercely
obviously	readily
apparently	rarely
intensely	extremely

13 How Things are Done

1 Criss-cross words

Ten list words are contained in the criss-cross below. Use the letters already given as a guide to you in identifying the ten words.

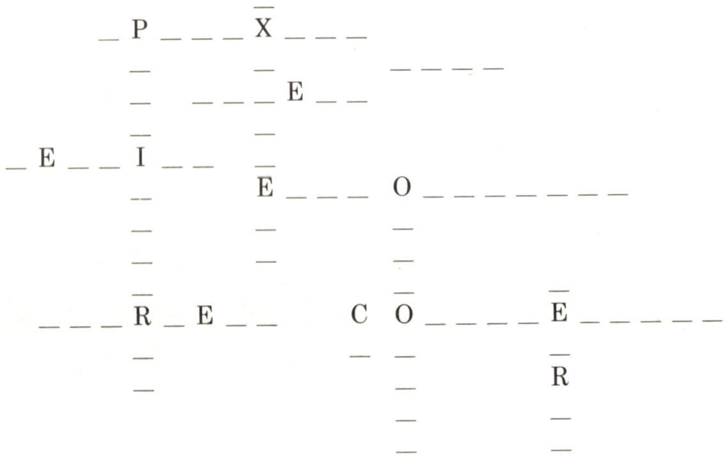

2 Use the clues!

(a) Your mum or dad is in its middle.

(b) Begins with a backwards dear.

(c) Jumbled green up front.

(d) Backwards trap at the start.

(e) An Australian friend near the end.

(f) Starts with a jumbled kind of trick.

(g) Ends with a jumbled salad vegetable starting with 'c'.

(h) Ends merely jumbled.

(i) Starts with a jumbled metal.

(j) Has an air hole after the start.

3 Words and meanings

Each list word below is surrounded by four possible meanings. Identify the correct meaning for each word.

(a) like a parent — truthfully

APPARENTLY

like a ghost — seemingly

(b) casually — steadily

ECONOMICALLY

thriftily — gradually

(c) in a strong manner — deliberately

INTENSELY

in a way that can be understood — in a successful manner

(d) specially — unfairly

PARTICULARLY

violently — unreasonably

(e) in a lively manner — ultimately

EVENTUALLY

comprehensively — equally

4 Mystery word

(a) Use the letters already provided to help you fill in the blanks below, and so identify one list word for each line across the table.

(b) Take the letters in the dark squares and arrange them to find the mystery list word.

Mystery word: ____________________

5 Word families

Complete the word families for the following list words by filling in the blanks in the table below.

	NOUN	VERB	ADJECTIVE	ADVERB
(a)				considerably
(b)				equally
(c)				economically
(d)				approximate
(e)				regularly

6 Blankety blanks

Choose the most appropriate list word to complete the blank in each of the sentences below.

(a) Comets .... appear in the sky.

(b) The team was .... careful about conceding penalties.

(c) The police will find out .... who committed the crime.

(d) The dog sprang .... into the attack.

(e) The reward was divided .... among the three children.

(f) The contest was an .... absorbing one.

(g) The government was at pains to follow an .... sound policy.

(h) .... one half of the residents have flourishing orchards.

7 Word wheels

Each word wheel below contains two list words. Experiment to find your starting letter for each word, and then find the rest of the word by taking every *second* letter, moving clockwise.

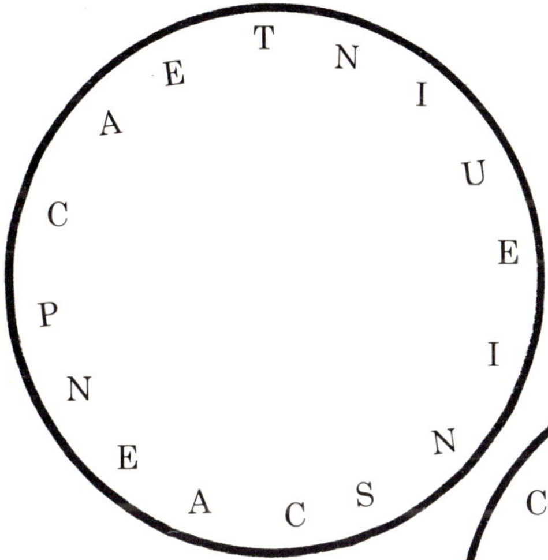

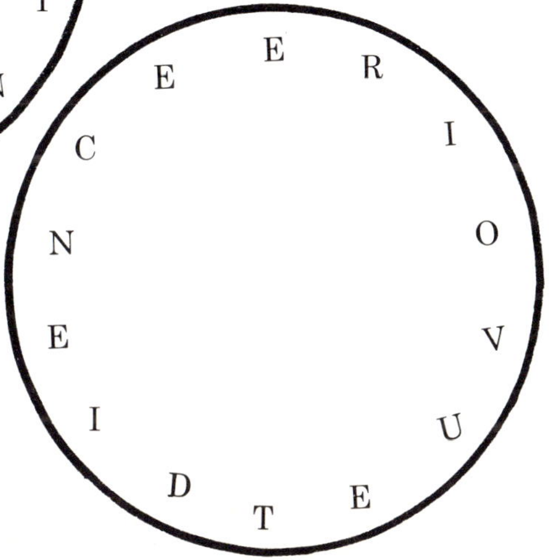

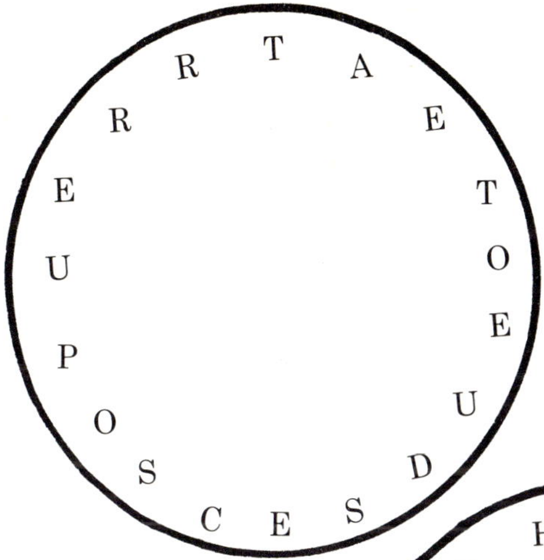

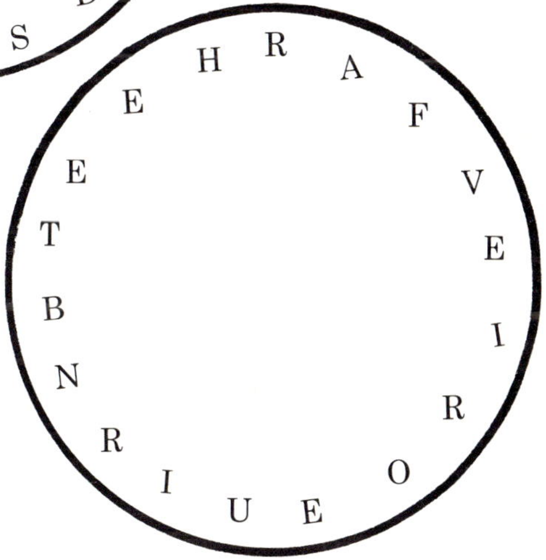

experience	reliable
confidential	conditions
employer	opportunity
vacancy	manager
career	position
reference	certificate
appointment	information
impression	efficient
interview	casual
temporary	apprentice

14 Going for a Job

1 Blanks

Use the list words to complete the blanks in the paragraph below.

reference	information
efficient	reliable
experience	position
vacancy	manager
appointment	impression
certificate	interview

When a .... occurs you must write to the .... to make an .... for an .... for the .... It is important that you make a good initial .... You should take a school .... or .... with any relevant information about you. Most employers like to take on someone who has had some .... and who is .... and ....

2 Criss-cross word

Ten list words are contained in the criss-cross below. Use the letters already given as a guide to you in identifying the ten words.

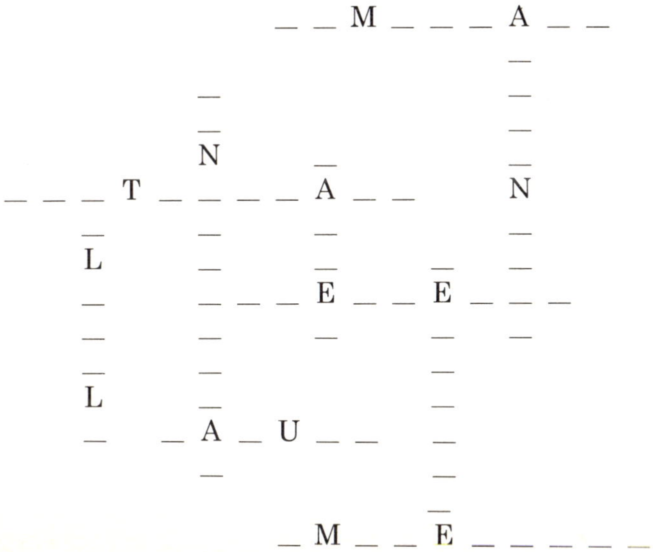

3 Design an advertisement

Work out two newspaper advertisements, each containing five different list words.

EXAMPLE: **Position** vacant; **efficient manager** for a large chain store; must have **experience**; excellent **conditions**.

4 Use the clues!

Find the list word suggested by each of the following clues.

(a) Has a confused romp in its middle.

(b) First five letters are the same whichever way you look at them.

(c) Without 'o', the end is a confused reply.

(d) To iron clothes in the middle.

(e) A dot in the middle.

(f) Has the place where a ship calls near its beginning.

(g) Jumbled short form of Trevor in the middle.

(h) A slang horse in the middle.

(i) Begins with chemical symbol for calcium.

(j) What you pay to use someone else's property in its middle.

5 Star-words

Each of the following star-words contains four list words with a common letter in the middle. By using one letter for each space along the lines (starting from the number each time), and using the letters already provided, find the words that fill out each star. One word is already completed in the first star.

4.
2. 3. E
_ _ M
_ _ P
_ _ L
1. _ _ M _ **O** _ _ _ _
Y _ _
E T M
R _ _
N _
_ _
_ _
_ _

2. 3.
_ _
_ _ 4.
T P _
_ _ _
1. _ _ F _ **R** _ N _ _
E _ _
_ _ I
_ _ _
_ _
_

6 Words and meanings

Find the correct meaning in the second column for each word in the first column.

	WORD	MEANING
(a)	conditions	event that affects someone
(b)	efficient	effect produced
(c)	reference	lasting for a limited time
(d)	impression	circumstances
(e)	confidential	written information about someone
(f)	vacancy	capable
(g)	experience	unoccupied position
(h)	temporary	entrusted with secrets

7 Completing

Use the correct form of the list word to complete each of the following sentences.

(a) The young typist had an .... list of references. [impression]

(b) One of the key qualities of a good manager is .... [efficient]

(c) She chose an .... time to begin computer studies. [opportunity]

(d) The firm had to .... the premises while renovations were carried out. [vacancy]

(e) She was offered a .... position at a high salary. [manager]

(f) He .... that they were looking for someone to promote. [confidential]

(g) It appears increasingly difficult to find stable .... in this town. [employer]

(h) The .... board did all in their power to make more positions available. [apprentice]

8 Word wheels

Each word wheel below contains two list words. Experiment to find your starting letter, then find the rest of the word by taking every *second* letter, moving clockwise.

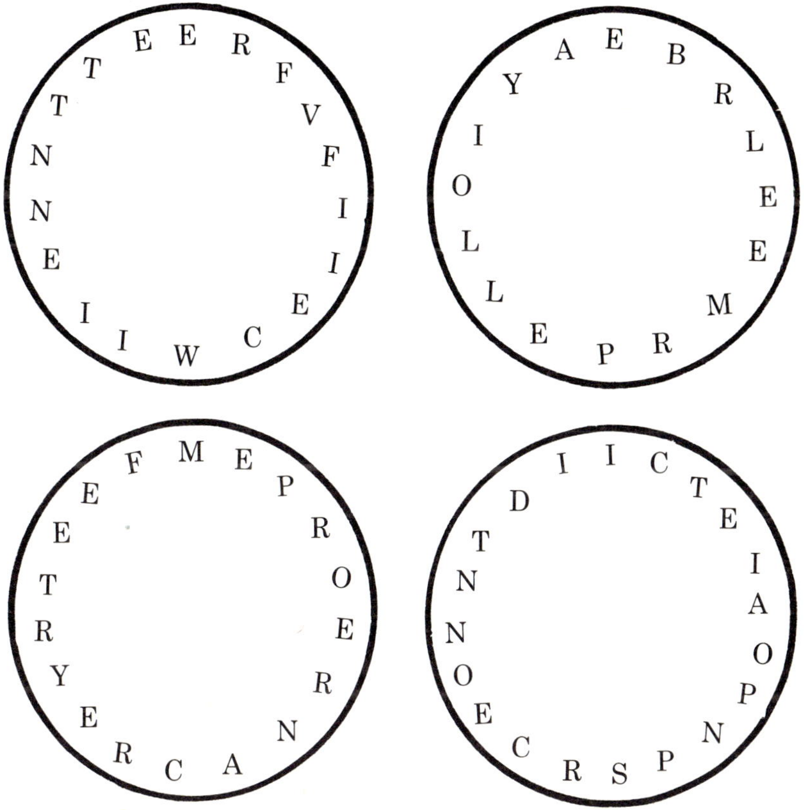

Spellbound's Noughts and Crosses Game

RULES

(1) The teacher (or a class member) draws up onto the blackboard a noughts and crosses grid, one metre by one metre.

(2) The teacher gives each of the nine squares a topic taken from the spelling units in this book. For each new game, the topics are rubbed out and new ones inserted.

(3) Each member of the class (except for the two contestants) is allocated a topic from the spelling book, and should turn to the appropriate page so that the contestants can be asked to spell words from the list.

Game In Progress

About People	*Life. Be in it.*	*The Trendy Teens*
Cashing In	*Spellbinder One*	*Face to Face*
Maths	*Now, Then, Soon*	*Going Places*

(4) One of the best ways of playing the game is to divide the class into two teams. Then for each game, a contestant is selected from each group. The names of the contestants who are to play against each other in a game can be taken from a hat.

(5) *The Game Begins*
First of all, the two contestants select a piece of chalk. They are going to play a game of noughts and crosses, but they will only be allowed to put up a nought or cross when they spell a word correctly. The teacher tosses a coin to see who will go first and the person who wins the toss will chalk up crosses and the opponent will chalk up noughts. The contestant who is having first go selects his topic (e.g. *Going Places*) from the grid. The student in the class who is looking after *Going Places* asks the contestant a word from the *Going Places* list. If the contestant spells the word correctly, a cross is put in the *Going Places* box in the grid. If the contestant spells the word incorrectly, no cross is allowed. Whatever happens, it now becomes the noughts contestant's turn, and the same process is repeated. Obviously, a box with a cross or a nought or cross in it cannot be used again. A box without a nought or cross can be used until one of the contestants is able to spell its word correctly. Succeed or fail, each contestant is allowed only one go at a time, as in noughts and crosses. Let the game begin!

Spelling Bingo

The teacher or student in charge of the game selects any three spelling lists from *Spellbound Two*—for example, *About People*, *Television*, and *Face To Face*. Then each member of the class writes down any ten words from these three lists in the form of a card. (It is better to put them in alphabetical order.)

challenge	popular
desperate	producer
dissatisfied	resistance
enthusiasm	society
featuring	sympathy

The teacher or person organizing the game now writes down the sixty words on small pieces of paper and places them in a hat or whatever container is available. He then draws out a word, reads it out and spells it. He does this for all sixty words. The students tick each word as it is called, if it is on their list. When a student has ticked off all of his ten words, he calls out 'Bingo!' and wins the game.

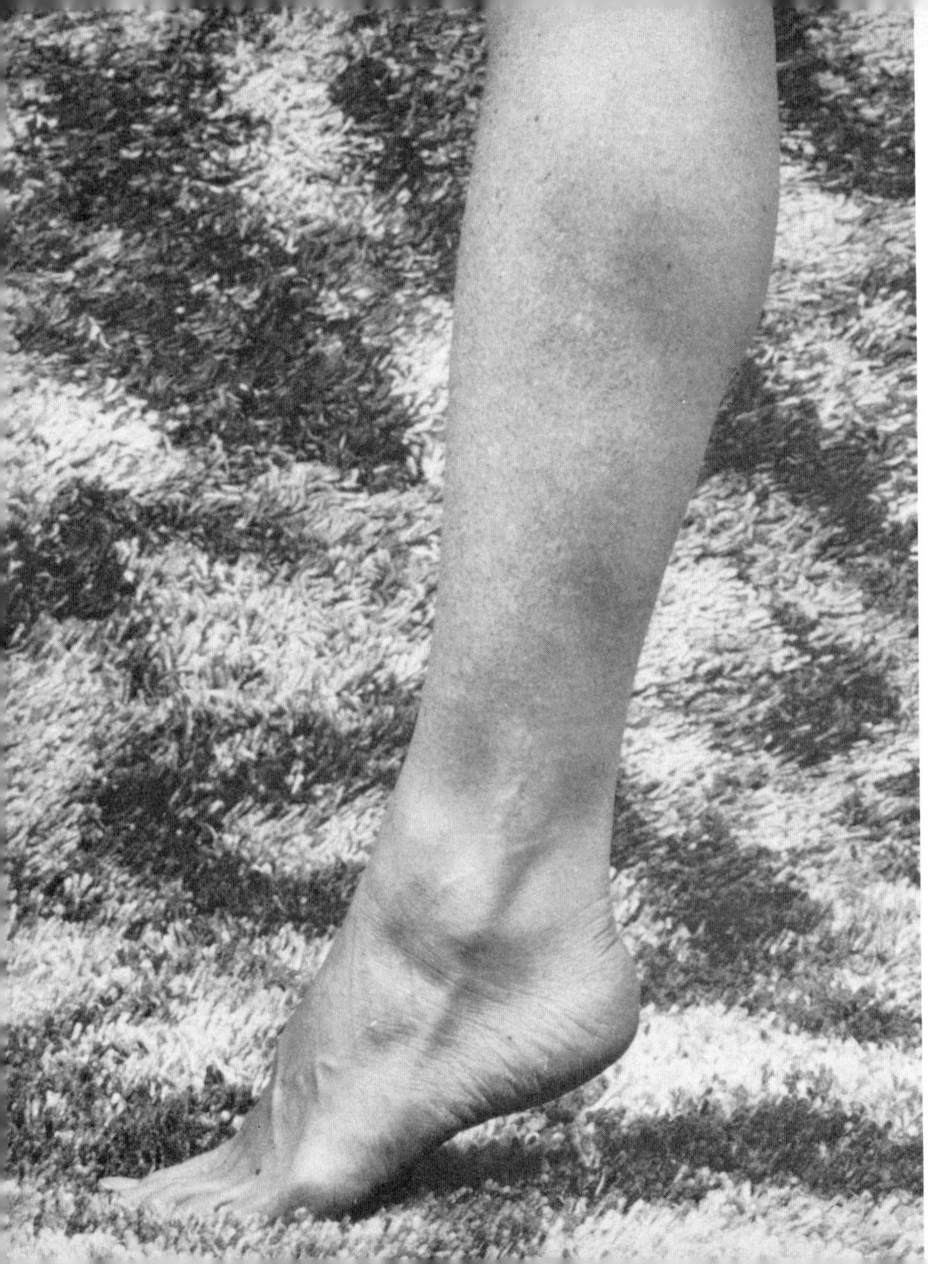

15 SPELLBINDER THREE

fascinate	exaggerate
improve	encourage
accompany	distribute
hesitate	support
disappear	interrupt
participate	persuade
transfer	influential
recommend	proceed
establish	comfortable
disappoint	opposite

1 Taking it lying down

Read through the following passage, filling in the blanks with *fourteen* of the list words as you go.

Last night I was just about to .... past the local high class restaurant when I saw something out of the corner of my eye on the .... side of the road that made me ....

Unable to believe what I saw, I looked away quickly hoping it would .... It would not. Now, it takes a lot to .... me, but the sight of an obviously ...., expensively dressed lady lying by the gutter did the trick.

Believe me, I do not .... when I say she looked almost .... flat on her back gazing up at the stars. Apparently, her exclusive blue-grey tint needed no .... apart from the road surface.

Going up to her, I cleared my throat so as not to .... her thoughtful mood too suddenly. Then I said, 'Excuse me, I wonder if I can .... you to seek medical advice? If you like, I'll .... you to a doctor. There's one nearby whom I can strongly ....'

'Thank you,' said the lying-down-lady coldly. 'I'm sorry to .... you, but I have no need of a doctor. I am simply reserving a parking space for my husband's Rolls Royce.'

2 Verbs — nouns

Write down the nouns from these verbs. Some of the verbs have two corresponding nouns.

	VERB	NOUN(S)
(a)	exaggerate	
(b)	accompany	
(c)	proceed	
(d)	hesitate	
(e)	transfer	
(f)	interrupt	
(g)	disappear	
(h)	fascinate	
(i)	encourage	
(j)	persuade	
(k)	establish	
(l)	participate	
(m)	distribute	
(n)	support	
(o)	improve	
(p)	recommend	
(q)	disappoint	

3 Synonym

A synonym is a word which has a similar meaning to another word. Line up the correct synonym for each of the following list words.

	LIST WORD	SYNONYM
(a)	proceed	vanish
(b)	hesitate	relaxing
(c)	disappear	go
(d)	transfer	powerful
(e)	establish	send
(f)	support	falter
(g)	comfortable	build
(h)	persuade	urge
(i)	influential	help

4 Snakes alive

Where the list words twine together, certain letters are revealed. Otherwise you're on your own.

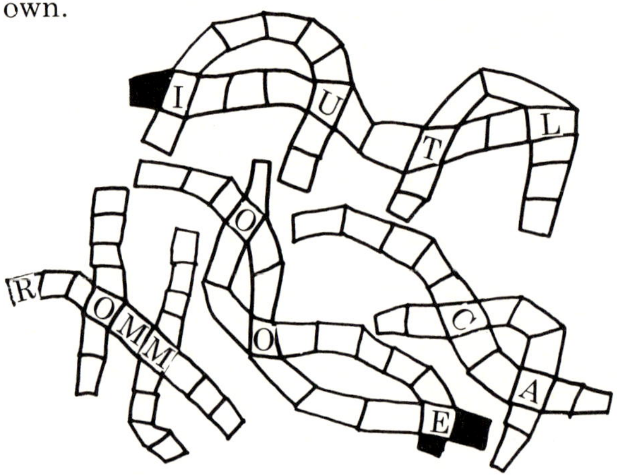

5 The INs and ATEs

Supply list words for the following.

(a) The very interesting ATE.

(b) The IN that has power.

(c) The unsure ATE.

(d) The IN that breaks in.

(e) The ATE that gets involved.

(f) The ATE that does not always tell the truth.

6 Cross letters

The list words forming the crosses share the encircled letter. Find these generous list words.

_
_
_
_
_
_
_
_
_
_ _ _ _ _ _ _ **E** _ _ _ _ _ _ _ _
_
_
_
_
_
_
_
_

_
_
_
_
_
_
_
_
_ _ _ _ _ _ **D** _ _ _ _ _ _ _ _
_
_
_
_
_
_
_
_
_

7 Fall outs

In each of the exercises that follow, two words from the list have been fused. Let one word fall out according to instuctions, and discover both words from the list.

(a) A word that means 'to get better' falls out and you're left with a word that means 'not as good as you expected'.

D I I S M P A O R P O P I V N T E

(b) A word that means 'to go along with' falls outs and you're left with a word that means 'join in'.

A P C A R C O T C I I M N A A Y P P T E

(c) A word that means 'to help' falls out and leaves you with a word meaning 'to go'.

P S U R C P O O P E R T E D

(d) A word that means 'hand round' or 'give out' falls out and leaves a word that means 'involving hardship'.

C D O M I S T F R O I R A B L B U T E T E

(e) A word meaning 'to send to another place' falls out and reveals a word of some importance.

I N R T F A L U E N F T A E L I R S N

16 Way out in the Wilderness

leisure	difficulty
equipment	ravine
horizon	cascade
vegetation	descend
valley	essential
boundary	forest
compass	route
climber	isolation
landscape	obstacle
tranquillity	protection

1 Use the clues!

Find a word from the list to fit each clue.

(a) Ends with the bush grapes grow on.
(b) Has a backwards cat in its middle.
(c) Ends with the short form of utility truck.
(d) Has a sure ending.
(e) Has an old-fashioned pen in its middle.
(f) Begins with a 3-letter girl's name.
(g) Ends with a kind of relaxation.
(h) Ends with a kind of overtake.
(i) Has part of a tree in it.
(j) Has a jumbled tens in its middle.

2 Alphabetizing

Re-arrange the following list words into the order in which they would be found in the dictionary.

cascade	compass
isolation	valley
climber	equipment
essential	obstacle
vegetation	difficulty

3 Word families

Fill in the blanks and so complete the following table.

	NOUN	ADJECTIVE
(a)	leisure	
(b)		essential
(c)	tranquillity	
(d)	difficulty	
(e)	protection	
(f)	isolation	

4 Fill in the blanks

Use the list words to fill in the blanks and so complete the story.

horizon	difficulty
landscape	tranquillity
isolation	boundary
essential	equipment
compass	valley
climber	forest
route	

The .... had .... with his .... along the .... through the .... Of course, his most essential piece was his .... , especially with the .... he faced. As he neared the .... of the forest and looked toward the mountains, the .... changed dramatically. He was overcome with the .... A .... stretched out before him, reaching right to the ....

5 Mystery word

(a) Copy out the word frame below into your workbook.

(b) Use the letters already given, to help you work out each list word across in the frame below.

(c) Take the letters in the dark squares and re-arrange them to find another list word, which is the MYSTERY WORD!

Mystery word: ____________________

6 Word circles

Each word circle below contains two list words. Experiment to find the first letter for each word and when you find it, take every *second* letter, moving clockwise, to solve the whole word.

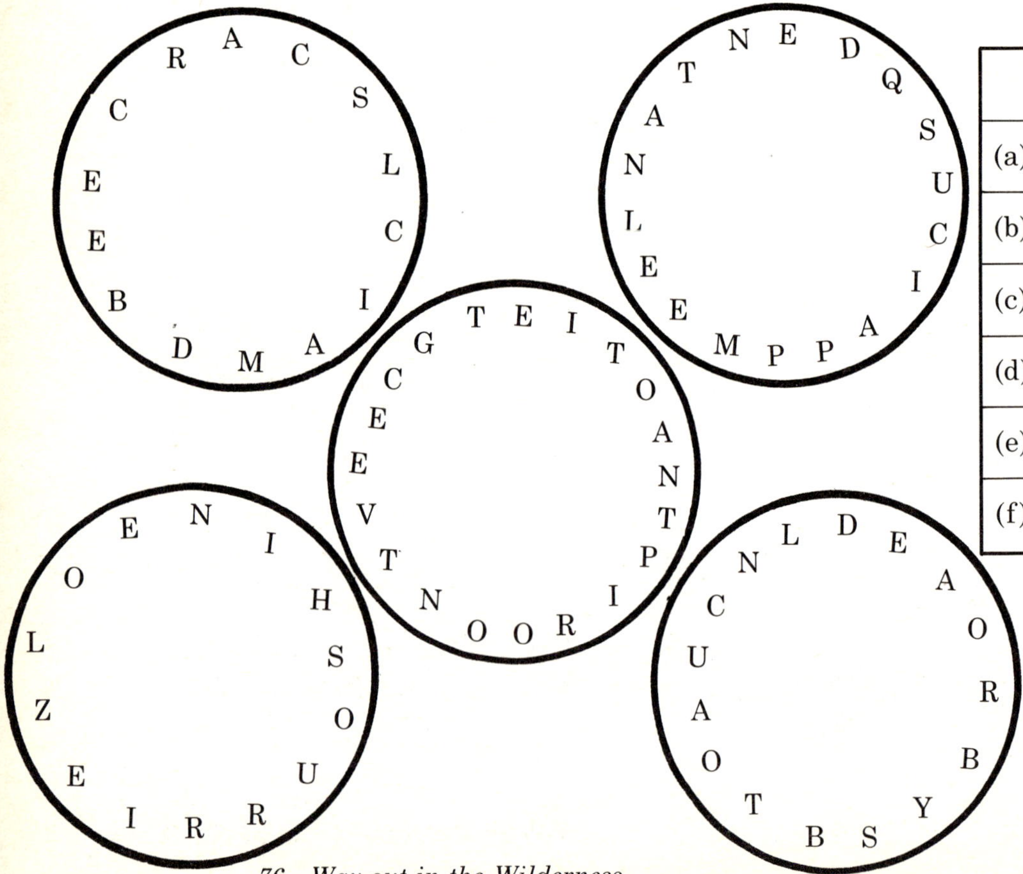

7 Antonyms (Opposites)

Column 1 contains jumbled antonyms (words opposite in meaning) to the list words in column 2. In your workbook, pair each list word with its correct antonym.

	ANTONYM	LIST WORD
(a)	desert	difficulty
(b)	ascend	leisure
(c)	turmoil	valley
(d)	ease	vegetation
(e)	work	tranquillity
(f)	mountain	descend

8 Jumbled syllables

Unjumble the syllables in the three columns below to find six list words.

One	Two	Three
tion	e	i
zon	hor	es
ial	sent	ment
ar	cle	y
ob	bound	tec
quip	pro	sta

cheque	finance
account	profit
deposit	lose
withdrawal	insurance
interest	scheme
business	contract
guarantee	borrow
available	apply
receipt	extravagant
balance	cashier
debt	

17 CASHING IN

1 Juggle words

Juggle the bracketed words so that they make sense in their sentences.

(a) Open a savings [**withdrawal**] with us and not only will you receive a very healthy rate of [**available**] per annum but you will also have the satisfaction of knowing that your money is readily [**interest**] for [**account**] whenever you need it.

(b) You have just placed money, that is you have made a [**cheque**], of money into your [**balance**] [**deposit**] which leaves you with a [**account**] of $100.

(c) If you wish to [**cashier**] money, first of all see the [**borrow**] and she will explain how our loan [**interest**] operates. You will, of course, have to pay [**borrow**] on the money you [**scheme**].

(d) In order to make a [**debt**] in your [**profit**] you must offer a product or service that everyone needs, and avoid getting into [**business**].

(e) If you are about to buy a house you must first of all have the [**contract**] and then sign a [**guarantee**] that will [**deposit**] honesty both for the buyer and the seller.

2 Forming up

Identify each of the following forms with a word from the list. To help you, some spaces and letters are given.

(a) _ _ _ _ _ _ _ _ _ _ _ *Number 15.*

Pay ________________________ $________

Signed

(b) ....

Received from..

the sum of..

with thanks..

(c) *Branch*..

Passbook No. ....

....

Received the sum of

.... $

(amount in words)

(d) *Signature of*..*or*

(e) ....

(f) *This household product is*
Fully ....*d*
against faulty workmanship
for a period of three months.

(g) ....

Branch..................................

Passbook No. ....

Amount.........................*ed*

(h) ....

Surname shown in passbook.

Cash		
Cheques		
Total $		

3 Fit-ins

Fit list words into the spaces. (NOTE: Some words may be used more than once.)

(a) __________ man to new secretary: 'I hear you wish to ______ for a position in our _________ department. How is your punctuation?'
New secretary (indignantly): 'I've never been late for work in my life.'

(b) ____________ official to car owner: 'No, sir, we can't make any money __________ to you if you _____ your car. However, we do ____________ to replace your car on _________ of your ____________ policy.'
Car owner: 'Mmmm. Well, I'll go along with the car, but if this is the way you do things around here I want to cancel the policy on my wife.'

(c) High pressure salesman to __________ man: 'I am a book salesman and I have a hire purchase ________ here that will definitely not involve you in any _______________ expenditure. (Offering a paper.) If you'll just read and sign this __________ and later pay by ________ . . .'
__________ man (impatiently): 'What is it you're selling? Come to the point. I'm a man of few words.'
Salesman: 'Just the man I'm looking for. My specialty is dictionaries.'

4 Ie or ei?

The spelling rule is: when *ie* or *ei* is pronounced as *ee*, the *i* comes before the *e* except after *c*.

believe → *ie*
receive → *ei*

(NOTE: There are some exceptions to the rule, e.g. 'weird' and 'seize'.)

(a) Find a list word that illustrates the *ie* part of the rule, and another one that illustrates the *ei* part.

(b) Use the rule to help you put *ie* or *ei* into the following words.

rel__ve
dec__t
conc__ve
s__ve
n__ce
conc__ve
s__ge

5 Coin a word

The 'coins' below will form word families if you can select the right part of speech for the right space. Here are all the words you need. Try fitting them into the right spaces.

financier
applicable
accountancy
finance
accountant
profit
profitable
application
applicant
profiteer
financially
profitably
financial

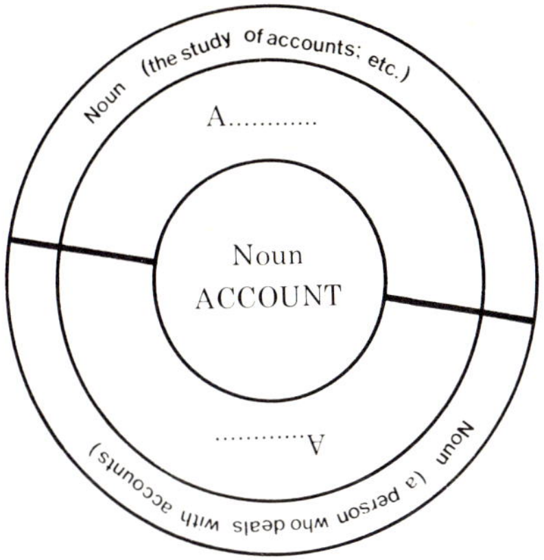

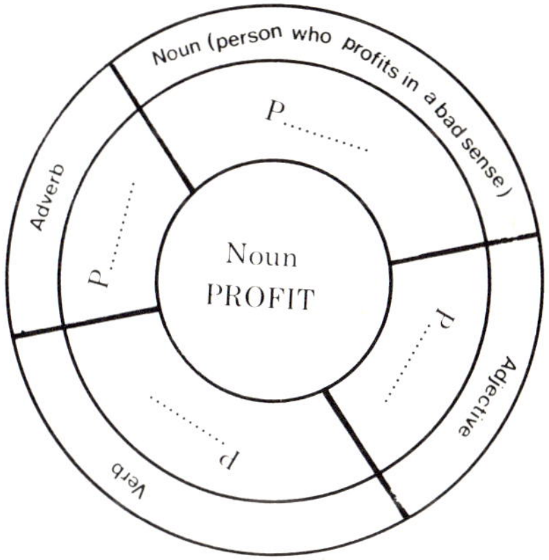

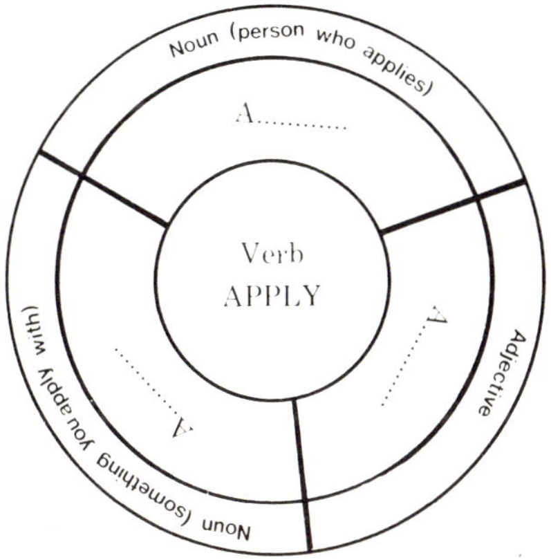

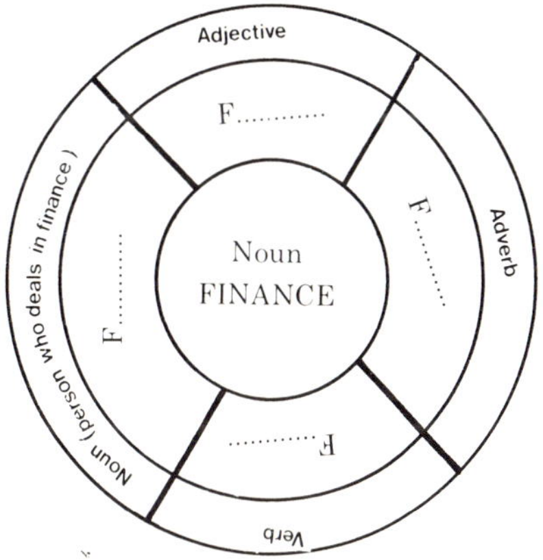

6 Double dollars

You can make important list words appear in the dollars by using (a) the common letters given and (b) the spaces that are available for other letters.

7 Coin connections

Money words are connected by having letters in common. Find the words.

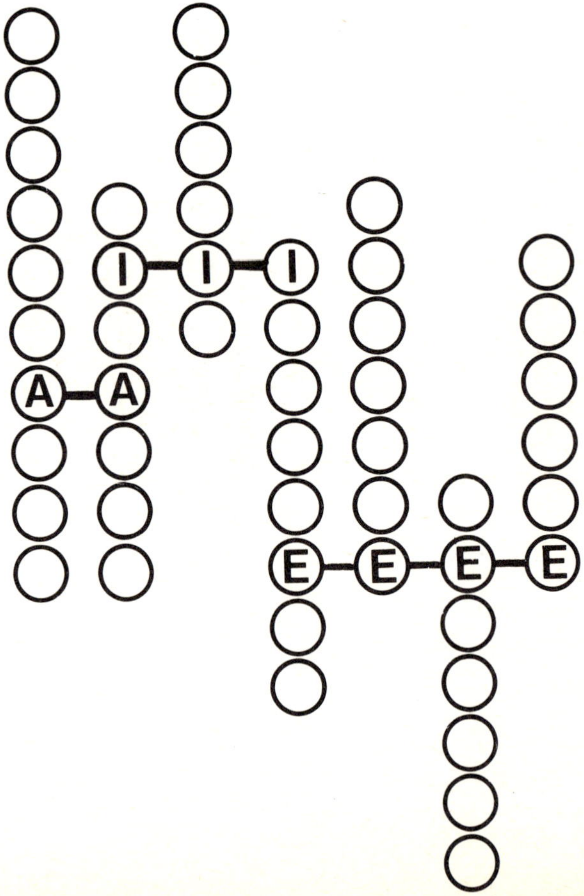

18 *In Your Neighbourhood*

pensioner	citizen
politician	suburb
lawyer	association
plumber	occupation
technician	charity
community	committee
neighbour	private
introduce	councillor
social	priest
rubbish	minister

1 Scrambled words

Unscramble each of the six list words below. Then, using the circled letters, form a seventh list word.

(a) e l r m b u p

(b) g u b r o h n e

(c) l o s i c a

(d) t i p r a e v

(e) r a l w e y

(f) u u b b r s

2 Finding another word

These words are other forms of list words. Complete them.

(a) technic__ __

(b) associat__ __

(c) priv__ __ __

(d) commun__ __

(e) occup__ __ __

(f) introduc__ __ __ __

3 Clues

Use the clues to discover the list words.

(a) The end of this word is the way some people say yes.

(b) The past tense of eat is the end of this word.

(c) Drop the first letter of this word and you have another name for timber.

(d) The last part of this word is very important when you play golf.

(e) The first part of this word used to be a very important piece of writing equipment.

(f) Tap is spelled backwards in the middle of this word.

(g) The name of an animal which is considered stupid begins this word.

(h) The middle of this word has the past tense of tread in it.

(i) The first part of this word has the sound a horse makes.

(j) The first part of this word happens when you use a towel.

4 Completing

Look at the word in brackets at the end of each sentence. Then use the correct form of this word in the sentence.

(a) .... is often considered a difficult profession. [politician]

(b) The local .... had to make a decision as to whether it would increase the rates. [councillor]

(c) .... and .... are very important people in our society. [priest, minister]

(d) .... living is very pleasant in Australia. [suburb]

(e) Many aged citizens live in our .... [neighbour]

(f) He wrote some .... comments on the report. [introduce]

(g) Some politicians are closely .... with a number of .... [association, charity]

(h) All .... in Australia provide social services. [community]

5 Selecting words

Select the correct words from the box and place them in the spaces provided.

plumber	social
pensioner	charity
lawyer	committee
occupation	rubbish

(a) His .... was that of a teacher.

(b) Our community has .... problems.

(c) A .... rather than a .... is needed to fix a leaking pipe.

(d) A .... was elected to work out a plan for reducing the amount of .... left in the streets.

(e) A .... obtains money for underprivileged people.

(f) The invalid .... had difficulty getting off the train.

6 What's my word?

My first is in pull
But not in full;
My second's in term
And also in first;
My third sounds like eye
And crops up in pie;
My fourth is in verse
But not in worse;
My fifth is in stay
And also in sway;
My sixth is in neat
And is something we eat;
My last is in trouble
And also in double;
My whole on a sign
Is 'Keep Out! It's mine'.

7 Match the meanings

Write down the list words and match them with meanings from the second column.

	LIST WORD	MEANING
(a)	committee	a person who receives fixed payments of money from a government or other institution
(b)	suburb	the giving of money and help
(c)	politician	group of people living in the same area
(d)	pensioner	a person engaged in public affairs
(e)	community	not public
(f)	introduce	organized body of people
(g)	charity	outlying district of a city
(h)	councillor	people appointed for a special function usually by a larger group of people
(i)	association	make known; bring forward
(j)	private	a person who serves on a council

8 Crossword

ACROSS

1. Many students enjoy going to a school ....
3. Students at .... schools have to pay fees.
6. The garbage man picks this up.
7. Almost every .... has a school and a church.

DOWN

2. We should all try to help our favourite ....
3. A man who administers the last rites.
4. A person whom you are meeting for the first time usually .... herself.
5. A man of the church.

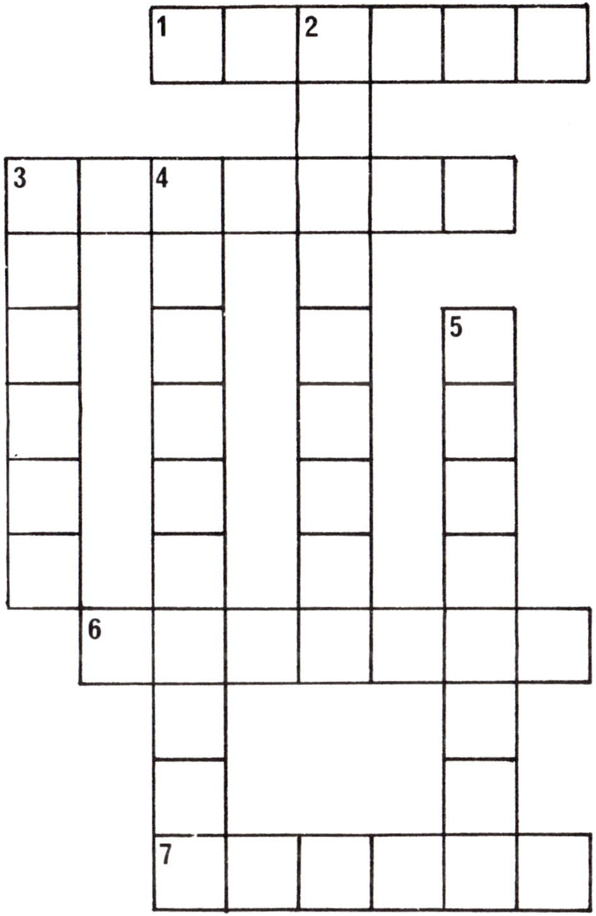

19 SPELLBINDER FOUR

victory	authority
representative	creature
quarrel	according
manufacture	expansion
kerosene	extension
instrument	column
innocent	majority
invisible	aborigine
familiar	privilege
invention	suspense

1 Clues

Use these clues to help you identify and write down words from your list.

(a) The middle of this word is an instrument that is used in cooking.

(b) The middle of this word is an alcoholic beverage that pirates used to like to drink.

(c) The middle of this word is a string with which you can move blinds up and down.

(d) Take away the first two letters and the last letter of this word and you have a word meaning 'the beginning'.

(e) The middle of this word is a writing instrument.

(f) The middle of this word is a beautiful flower that has thorns on its branch.

(g) The middle of this word is something we like to receive on our birthday.

(h) The middle of this word is something beginning with 'v' that lets air in and out.

(i) This word ends with a coin used in Australian currency.

(j) The first six letters of this word form the name of a person who writes books.

2 Completing

Use the words from the list to complete the sentences.

(a) The fog caused the oncoming traffic to be ....

(b) Some people consider the opportunity to vote to be a ....

(c) The businessman was involved in the .... of car accessories.

(d) The dingo is a .... which is troublesome to farmers.

(e) It is best not to .... over trivial matters.

(f) .... is often used for heating.

(g) Today an aeroplane flight is a .... to some people.

(h) .... to Einstein, $E = mc^2$.

3 Scrambled words

Three words from the list have been mixed up in the box. Find the three words.

E S u U c l i T S y s

M N E M d o j r o a n

4 Match the meanings

Match the words in the left-hand column with the correct meanings in the right-hand column.

(a) victory	greater number
(b) quarrel	advantage, right
(c) instrument	disagreement, dispute
(d) familiar	anxious, uncertainty
(e) authority	winning
(f) majority	close, friendly
(g) privilege	not able to be seen
(h) suspense	power over others
(i) invention	tool, implement
(j) invisible	new device

5 Missing words

Use the correct forms of the list words in the brackets to complete the sentences.

(a) He was a .... child. [quarrel]

(b) Edison .... the electric light. [invent]

(c) Some people say that .... breeds contempt. [familiar]

(d) Some .... believe that the motor car is harmful to our well being. [authority]

(e) The Australian soldiers were .... at Tobruk. [victory]

(f) The prisoner's .... was obvious to the judge. [innocent]

(g) The builder .... the laundry. [extension]

(h) The .... coastal cities of Australia are heavily populated. [majority]

(i) All the students' .... were .... [privilege, suspense]

(j) He had .... Peru at the Olympic Games. [representative]

6 Opposites

Write down the opposites of these words.

(a) innocent (b) victory

(c) majority (d) expansion

(e) invisible (f) familiar

7 Complete the words

The incomplete words are from your list. Write them down in your books.

(a) _nn_____

(b) ____i_i__

(c) s_s___s_

(d) _cc______

(e) _re___re

(f) i__i_i___

(g) ___rr__

(h) _e___e_e

8 Verbs

Write down the verbs from the following words (e.g. attraction — attracts).

(a) expansion (b) suspense

(c) representative (d) invention

(e) extension (f) familiar

(g) authority

20 *Plaza, Mall And Shopping Centre*

department	assistant
customer	hairdresser
jeweller	counter
pharmacy	selection
cafeteria	articles
display	elevator
purchase	retail
advertisement	hardware
chemist	nursery
afford	facilities

1 Use the clues!

Find a word from the list above to fit each of the following clues.

(a) Begins with a hospital employee.

(b) Has a jumbled times in its middle.

(c) You could draw water from the middle of this word.

(d) Has a 3-letter boy's name in the middle.

(e) Starts with a donkey.

(f) Has a kind of fair or bazaar in its middle.

(g) Ends in a kind of fog.

(h) Has a portion in its middle.

(i) Contains an article of clothing.

(j) Ends in backwards rot.

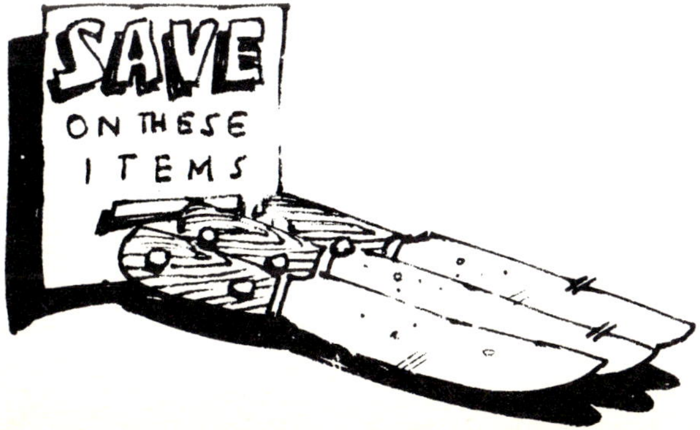

2 Word circles

Each circle of letters contains two list words. Once you find the first letter of the word, you work out the word by taking every *second* letter, moving clockwise.

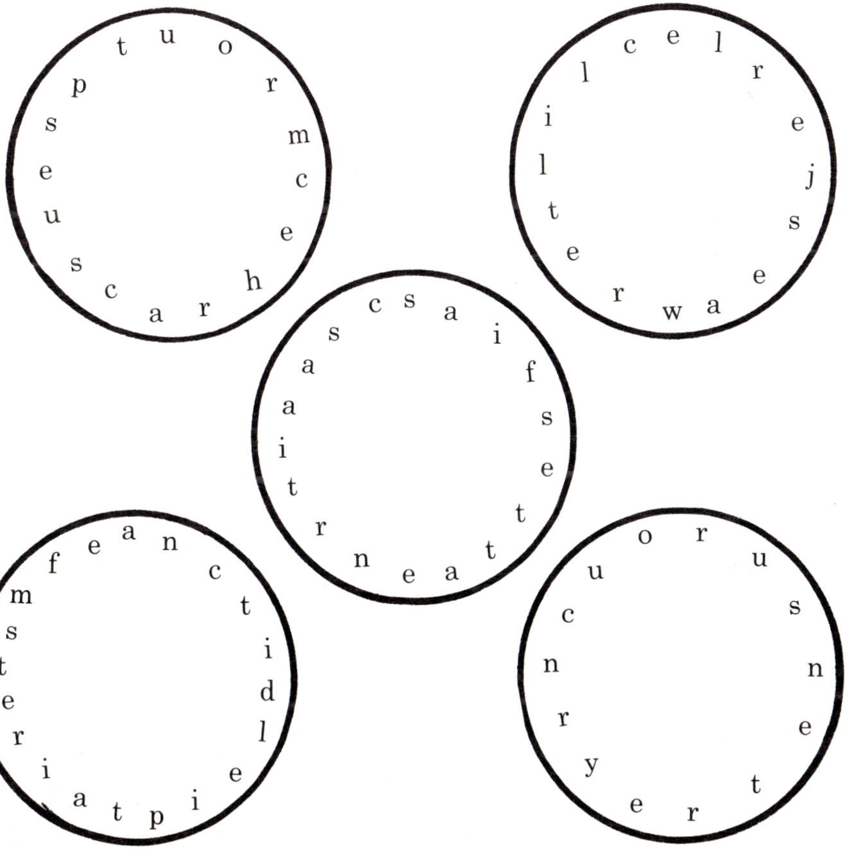

3 What is the word?

Find the list word that fits each of the following definitions.

(a) A place that sells young plants.

(b) To buy.

(c) Someone who purchases goods.

(d) One section of a large store.

(e) To put goods on show.

(f) To sell goods.

(g) A place that provides light meals.

(h) Person who helps you with your purchase.

(i) Facility that transports you from one floor to another.

4 Missing letters

Every third letter of the following list words is provided. Find the missing letters, and so work out the words.

(a) _ _ r _ _ a _ _	(b) _ _ t _ _ l _ _
(c) _ _ p _ _ t _ _ n _	(d) _ _ v _ _ t _ _ e _ _ n _
(e) _ _ e _ _ s _	(f) _ _ a _ _ a _ _
(g) _ _ f _ _ e _ _ a	(h) _ _ r _ _ a _ _

5 Mystery word

(a) Each line across in the table below is a list word. Use the letters given as clues to help you find the words.

(b) Take the letters in the dark squares and re-arrange them to find the mystery word.

Mystery word: _ _ _ _ _ _ _

		■	R		R					
		C		■		T				
		F		■			I			
E		■	V							
		U			E	■				
■		F	O							

6 Fill in the blanks

hairdresser	advertisement
purchase	department
assistant	afford
customer	pharmacy
elevator	counter

Use the list words above to fill in the blanks in the passage below.

The .... saw the .... on the .... of the .... where she made her .... of shampoo and talcum powder. She went up the .... to see if the new .... and his .... could give her a new style that she could .... with her housekeeping money.

7 Criss-cross word

Copy the diagram below into your workbook. Then use the clues to help you complete the criss-cross word.

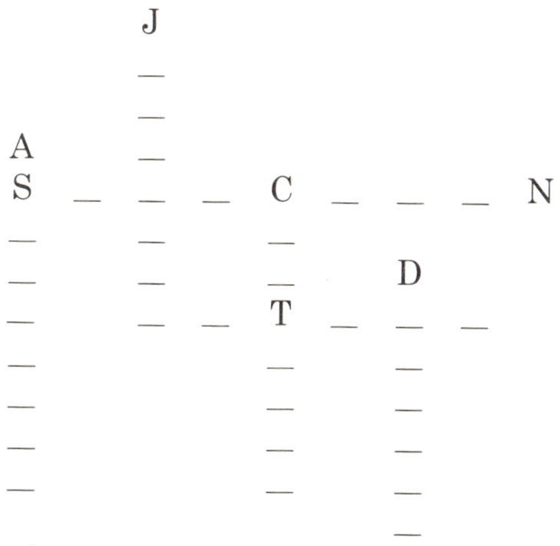

CLUES
A —a helper
S —choice
C —shopper
D —show

8 Spell-a-word

Divide the class into pairs and draw up score sheets like the ones below.

Player 1	Player 2
Points 1111 Errors:	Points 1111 Errors: diary

RULES

(1) Player 1 chooses a word from the list for his partner to spell. If it is spelt correctly, player 2 wins a point. If it is spelt incorrectly, player 1 wins a point.

(2) In his turn, player 2 does the same. Scoring is the same.

(3) Note spelling errors as they occur. When all the words have been asked once, each player has two minutes to review his errors. Then he or she has to spell all errors.

coarse	principle
course	principal
waist	gorilla
waste	guerilla
peace	sight
piece	site
allowed	lose
aloud	loose
current	hoarse
currant	horse
weather	stationary
whether	stationery

21 CONFUSING DOUBLES

1 Simplify the pairs

Select the correct pairs from the box for each of the sentences, and then make sure you put them in their correct positions.

principal principle	horse hoarse
site sight	aloud allowed
lose loose	waste waist
weather whether	stationary stationery

(a) Do not .... that .... screw from the wood.

(b) I do not know .... the .... will improve.

(c) He left his .... car to buy some ....

(d) The new school building .... was a wonderful .... for the headmaster.

(e) The girl was not .... to speak .... in the classroom.

(f) The girl became .... after she commanded her .... to stop galloping.

(g) The .... of the school believed in the .... of free speech.

(h) A large .... line often shows that you do not .... food.

2 Clues

Use the clues provided to write down list words.

(a) The middle of these two list words has something that is used in rowing.

(b) The end of this word is a little insect which likes sugar.

(c) The end of this word means the opposite of soft.

(d) The beginning of these two list words is a place where the trains stop.

(e) The beginning of this word is the plural of 'I'.

(f) The end of this word is something a good tennis player serves.

(g) The beginning of this word is something most of us enjoy eating.

(h) The beginning of this word is the opposite of stop.

(i) The end of this word describes what has happened after you have been to a church to be married.

(j) The end of this word is the fee you pay to the owner for the flat or house you're occupying.

3 Cracking the code

Take the shape formed by the lines around the letters as a code. [shape] = e, [shape] = a.

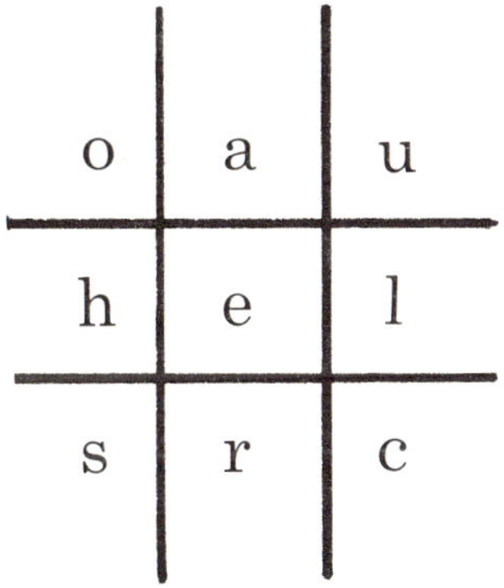

Now decode the following to form words from your list.

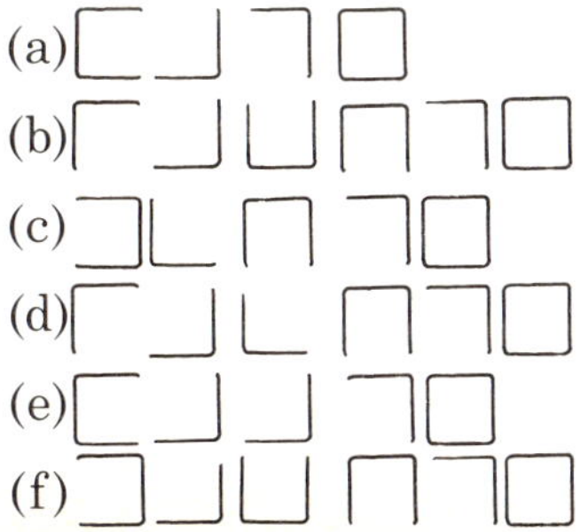

4 Where words come from

'Current' comes from the Latin word *curro*, I run. A current, electrical or otherwise, 'runs' along. There are many words in English coming from *curro*, 'I run'. They mostly have 'cur' within them. Work out the *curro* words from the 'cur' clues below.

(a)	c_ncur	to agree (run together)
(b)	r_cur	to happen again (run again)
(c)	exc_rsi_n	a journey out (running out of)
(d)	_ccur	to happen (run)
(e)	c_rr_ncy	money (it runs from hand to hand)
(f)	c_rs_ve	running writing

The cat sat on the mat.

5 Using the correct word

Look at the word in brackets at the end of each sentence. Then use the correct form of this word in the sentence.

(a) The new workman has been .... too much time. [waste]

(b) Captain Cook called the Pacific Ocean 'pacific' because it was so .... [peace]

(c) The author is .... her new book. [revise]

(d) The principal received a substantial .... for audio-visual equipment. [allowed]

(e) The train passenger has .... his ticket. [lose]

(f) The fisherman had .... five sharks. [sight]

(g) There are many .... you can attempt. [course]

(h) In the hot weather people should .... their ties. [loose]

6 Match the meanings

Match the list words with their meanings from the right-hand column.

(a)	stationary	head person
(b)	stationery	person engaged in irregular warfare
(c)	guerilla	rough
(d)	principal	permitted
(e)	principle	stopped
(f)	allowed	husky
(g)	hoarse	writing materials
(h)	sight	ground on which building stands or is to stand
(i)	site	fundamental truth
(j)	coarse	released
(k)	loose	seeing

7 Straight across words

Work out the seven Across words. One letter in each word has been given to help you. (7 Across has two answers.)

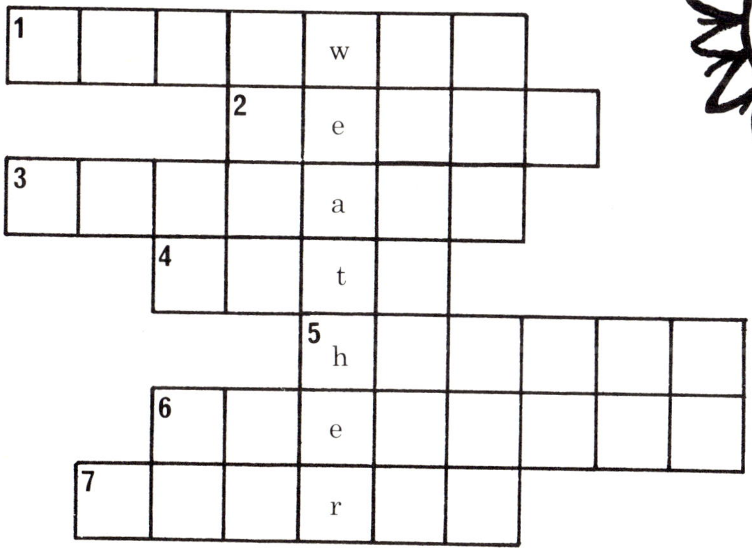

dictionary	analysis
illiterate	knowledge
sensible	explanation
example	error
studious	confusing
language	disobedient
expression	deliberately
absence	pronoun
enrolment	character
competition	corridor

22 CHALK TALK

1 Use the clues

Find a word from the list above to fit each of the following clues.

(a) The middle of this word is what you often call a small animal kept in your home.

(b) The end of this word is used in measuring things.

(c) The first part of this word is a shortened term for examination.

(d) The end of this word is something you should be careful not to fall off.

(e) The middle of this word is something you do when you want to use a lift. You .... the button.

(f) The first three letters of this word mean 'sick'.

(g) The end of this word is something a choir does.

(h) The end of this word is an abbreviation for sister.

(i) The middle of this word means to 'think ahead'.

(j) This word rhymes with 'fence'.

2 Match the meanings

Write down the list words and next to them put their correct meanings.

(a)	pronoun	on purpose
(b)	illiterate	mistake
(c)	absence	a making known of the facts
(d)	confusing	unable to read and write
(e)	error	being away
(f)	explanation	a word that stands in place of a noun
(g)	analysis	passageway in a building
(h)	disobedience	examination of the parts
(i)	deliberately	mixed up
(j)	corridor	act of not following orders

3 Missing words

Use the correct form of the list word in the brackets and insert it in the blank space in each of the following sentences.

(a) The teacher .... the student's progress. [analysis]

(b) The new teacher .... her plan to the class. [explanation]

(c) Each .... played well. [competition]

(d) A great deal of .... had come from the principal's decision. [confusing]

(e) The class needed thirty .... [dictionary]

(f) She .... read her novel. [studious]

(g) The student had been .... for five days. [absence]

(h) The rate of .... seems to be increasing. [illiterate]

(i) He had .... in the new photography course. [enrolment]

(j) The headmaster .... a desire to see the class captains. [expression]

4 Crossword

ACROSS

3. Something you give to your parents when you are late home at night.
7. Parents have to complete one of these before their children can start school.
8. The opposite of being able to read and write.
9. Something we try not to make when we are doing an exam.
10. This word rhymes with 'paralysis'.

DOWN

1. Teachers try to set a good ....
2. This book gives the meanings of thousands and thousands of words.
4. This is important in our communication with each other.
5. Teachers like their students to be ....
6. This word describes someone who likes reading books.

5 ABC

Four of your list words are mixed together so that all of their letters are arranged alphabetically. Can you unscramble the four words?

A A A B C D D E E E E I I

I L L L N N N N O O O O O

P P R R R R R T T U X Y

6 Word salad

Fifteen of your list words are in this word salad. The words occur horizontally, vertically and sometimes diagonally. Write down the fifteen words.

E	G	D	E	L	W	O	N	K	S	S
C	C	S	L	T	S	S	E	D	N	E
C	O	M	P	E	T	I	T	I	O	N
H	N	E	M	E	U	S	A	C	I	S
A	F	C	A	R	D	Y	R	T	S	I
R	U	N	X	R	I	L	E	I	S	B
A	S	E	E	O	O	A	T	O	E	L
C	I	S	E	R	U	N	I	N	R	E
T	N	B	R	R	S	A	L	A	P	E
E	G	A	U	G	N	A	L	R	X	C
R	E	N	R	O	L	M	I	Y	E	H

7 Ex

The prefix 'ex' means 'out of'. Using the meanings below, work out the missing letters and write down the words next to their meanings.

(a)	exh_l_	to breathe out
(b)	exp__t	to send out (goods)
(c)	exc_v_te	to dig out soil, leaving a hole
(d)	ex__	to go out
(e)	extr_ct	to take out
(f)	excl_d_	to shut out
(g)	excl__m	to cry out
(h)	ex_c_tion	the carrying out of a task

23 In Sickness and in Health

cough	illness
fracture	specialist
asthma	symptom
operate	complaint
contagious	diagnosis
infection	disease
paralyse	bandage
conscious	swollen
surgeon	hospital
injection	medicine

1 Clues

Use these clues to help you identify and write down words from your list.

(a) The beginning of this word is a musical performance.

(b) The middle of this word has something you'd never want to fall into.

(c) The beginning of this word is something that most golfers aim to do for each hole.

(d) This word ends in a man's name. (He stole a pig in a nursery rhyme.)

(e) This word ends with the slang expression meaning 'aren't'.

(f) The middle of this word is something you do on stage.

(g) The middle of this word is a little sound you make when you are giving a talk and you are unsure of what to say next.

(h) The last two letters of this word are sometimes used as an abbreviation for 'mother'.

(i) This word rhymes with 'delicious'.

(j) The end of this word has much to do with being comfortable.

2 Missing words

Use the correct form of the list word in the brackets, and insert it in the blank space in each of the following sentences.

(a) The child was .... [asthma]

(b) He lost .... during the accident. [conscious]

(c) There are still some .... which do not have a cure. [illness]

(d) The doctor had decided to .... in allergies. [specialist]

(e) The injured footballer was suffering from .... of the legs. [paralyse]

(f) Since the student's illness was .... he was not allowed to go to school. [infection]

(g) The surgeon quickly .... the antidote into the patient's vein. [injection]

(h) The boy .... his arm when he fell from the tree. [fracture]

3 Ough words

Complete the following sentences by inserting words with 'ough' in them. Sometimes the first letter is given to help you.

(a) The teacher said that he had just about had e............ .

(b) The ball went .... the fence.

(c) She fell from the .... of the tree.

(d) The cook mixed up the d............ .

(e) The sea had become very r............ .

(f) He .... many books with his money.

(g) The soldier f............ bravely.

(h) The teacher t............ a great deal about the student's problem.

(i) The accident victim s............ help from many car drivers.

(j) The patient had a nasty ....

(k) The horse was drinking from the t............ .

4 Jumbled letters

Unscramble the letters to make up words from your list.

(a) s i n t o o g u a c

(b) n i n i j o t c e

(c) h o g c u

(d) e w o l n s l

(e) i i s s d o a g n

(f) e e s s a d i

5 Completing

Use the words from the list to complete the sentences.

(a) .... is an illness which makes breathing difficult.

(b) The doctor tied a .... around the patient's .... leg.

(c) The general practitioner was unable to give a definite .... , so he sent his patient to a ....

(d) The .... was unwilling to .... until the accident victim was brought to the ....

(e) An .... in his lung caused the patient to .... frequently.

(f) Leprosy is a ....

6 Find the word

Use the clues to work out the list word.

My first is in panic
But not in trouble;
My second's in miss
And occurs as a double;
My third is in tan
But not in sun;
My fourth is in hand
And also in thumb;
My fifth is in hammer
But not in nail;.
My sixth is in boat
And also in sail;
I'm a condition no doubt
You'd be better without.

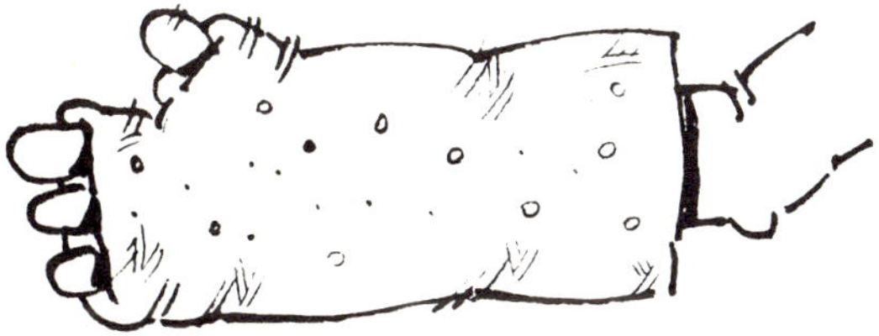

7 Match the meanings

Write down the words from the left-hand column and match them with the correct meanings from the right-hand column.

(a)	contagious	grown bigger
(b)	fracture	aware, mentally awake
(c)	paralyse	illness, sickness
(d)	swollen	identification of illness
(e)	diagnosis	catching (of disease)
(f)	surgeon	sign of existence of illness
(g)	conscious	breaking
(h)	injection	forcing liquid through syringe
(i)	symptom	to cripple, to make powerless
(j)	disease	a doctor who operates

8 Where words come from

The Latin word *opus* (*operis*) means 'a work'. Thus a doctor performs a medical 'work' when he operates. Write down the English words connected with *opus*. (Some letters are given to help you.)

	MEANING	WORD
(a)	To work together	c___er__e
(b)	A musical work	o____
(c)	Not able to be operated on	i___er___e

24 SPELLBINDER FIVE

bachelor	massacre
electricity	signal
exception	religious
respectable	practical
witness	conference
industry	altitude
banana	compulsory
coffee	unfortunately
canoe	union
struggle	weapon

1 Clues

Use these clues to help you identify and write down words from your list.

(a) This word has a pain in it and begins with the name of a famous musician.

(b) The end of this word is like a town but much bigger.

(c) The end of this word has something you eat on.

(d) The middle of this word is a small carpet.

(e) The end of this word means a payment.

(f) It is not good to get the middle of this word in your eyes or in electrical equipment.

(g) The first part of this word is part of some church services; the last part is a measurement of land.

(h) Change the first letter of this word to 'o' and you have a vegetable that stings your eyes when you peel it.

(i) The first part of the word means that you 'are able' to do something.

(j) This word has a fish in it beginning with 't'.

2 Mixed pieces

Make up *eight* of your list words by joining together pieces in the box.

oe	re
al	lig
wit	can
fer	ness
weap	sign
con	ious
able	re
on	ence
acre	mass
spect	

3 Completing

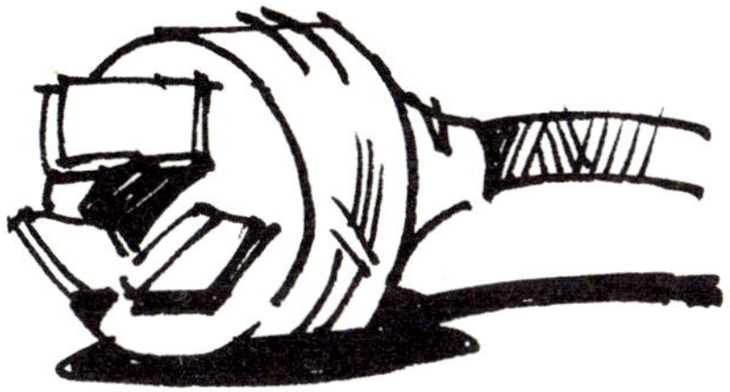

Use the words from your list to complete the sentences.

(a) .... the policeman was not able to make an .... to the rule.

(b) The .... tree needs a hot climate to grow well.

(c) Sometimes a high .... affects one's breathing.

(d) It is .... for all Australian car drivers to keep to the left.

(e) Suburban trains mostly rely on .... for their power.

(f) A .... was held for union leaders.

(g) .... is becoming more popular than tea in Australia.

(h) The .... from the stationmaster stopped the train.

4 Match the meanings

Write down the words in the first column. Next to them write their meanings from the second column.

(a) witness	of good social standing
(b) signal	person present at event
(c) altitude	branch of manufacture
(d) massacre	sign conveying direction or information
(e) compulsory	height
(f) religious	thing that does not follow the rule
(g) respectable	forced
(h) exception	believing in a system of worship
(i) bachelor	slaughter
(j) industry	unmarried man

5 Code

Take the shape formed by the lines around the letters as a code, e.g. a=⌋, c=□.

a	n	o
s	c	m
e	f	r

Now decode the following list words.

(a) 

(b) 

(c) 

(d) 

6 Jumbled equations

Find list words by solving the following equations and unjumbling the letters.

2e+c+2f+o=eecffo=coffee

(a) f+3e+2c+2n+ro=?

(b) 2a+2s+mc+re=?

(c) 3a+2n+b=?

(d) 2a+2c+tripe+l−e=?

(e) −a+2e+l+2t+ray+2i+2c=?

7 How words began

The word 'compulsory' or 'compel' suggests the idea of people being forced to do something. Actually the Latin word *pello* (*pulsus*) means 'to drive' or 'to hurl'.

Complete the table for these words coming from *pello* (*pulsus*). The first example has been done for you.

	VERB	NOUN	ADJECTIVE
(a)	compel	compulsion	compulsive
(b)	expel		
(c)	propel		
(d)	repel		
(e)	impel		

8 Missing words

Use the correct form of the list word in brackets and insert it in the blank space in each of the following sentences.

(a) The new gardener was very .... [industry]

(b) There were three .... to the accident. [witness]

(c) The fire in the television studio was caused by an .... fault. [electricity]

(d) The swimmer had been .... to leave the water. [compulsory]

(e) People seem to achieve more when they are .... [union]

(f) It was .... that the train had been delayed. [unfortunately]

(g) The doctor was .... to save the life of the injured man. [struggle]

(h) There are many different .... throughout the world. [religious]

25 Sweeping up the Leaves

moisture	level
gardener	improvement
fountain	boundary
cultivate	eucalyptus
fertile	barren
rubbish	fragrant
poisonous	lettuce
abundant	spinach
materials	cauliflower
beautiful	excavate

1 Grow-a-word

Grow 8-letter list words from the clues given. The clues are groups of letters (numbered to show (position) which form little words occurring within the list words. Find as many of these little words as you can and grow the list word from them. (In the first one, 2, 3, 4 has been done to help you.)

(a)

1	2	3	4	5	6	7	8
	B	U	N				

Letters: 2, 3, 4 : a kind of bread roll
5, 6, 7 : a boy's name
2, 6, 8 : used in a game
6, 7, 8 : a widespread insect

(b)

1	2	3	4	5	6	7	8

Letters: 1, 2, 8 : opposite of 'girl'
5, 6, 8 : when the sun is up
1, 6, 7 : found in a hotel

(c)

1	2	3	4	5	6	7	8

Letters: 1, 6, 8 : opposite of 'thin'
2, 3, 4 : an old bit of cloth
2, 3, 7, 8 : carry on in a loud voice

(d)

1	2	3	4	5	6	7	8

Letters: 3, 4, 5, 8 : dark hollow space in the ground
5, 6, 7 : a large tub
3, 4, 7 : a domestic pet (feline)

(e)

1	2	3	4	5	6	7	8

Letters: 3, 4 : a part of the verb 'to be'
3, 7, 8 : anger
1, 3, 4, 5 : a light rain or fog

(f)

1	2	3	4	5	6	7	8

Letters: 4, 5, 6 : a wild animal's lair
2, 3, 5 : a part of the verb 'to be'

(g)

1	2	3	4	5	6	7	8

Letters: 5, 6, 8 : a brownish colour
1, 6, 8 : to keep you cool
2, 3, 5 : exit

2 Seeds

Each 'seed' is composed of two list words; however, you are supplied with only two end letters for clues. At the left-hand end of the seed is the letter that *begins* one of the words, while at the right-hand end is the letter that *ends* the other word. See if you can crack the words.

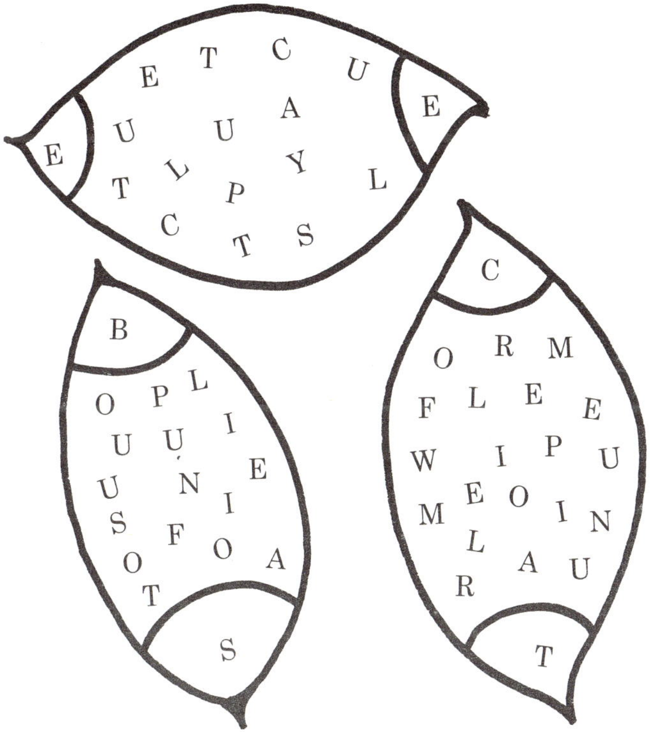

3 Up the garden path

All the list words will fit into one or other of the categories below. To help you, spaces show the number of words that will fit into each category. In addition, at least one vowel (a, e, i, o, or u) or consonant (all other letters of the alphabet apart from the vowels) is given.

WATERY	GROWTH	LANDSCAPING
___S____	________E	__V__
____T___	_E_____	__C_____
		_______L_
		___R_______
		_____A__
		__R_____

USELESS	NOURISHING/ MEDICINAL	JOY TO THE SENSES
___R__	__T____	____R___
____I__	____A__	______F__
______O__	_______O___	
	______P___	

4 Full to -ful

'Full' means as much as you can get of anything, but when it's added to the end of a word it drops an 'l'.

Full of beauty becomes beauti*ful*.

Write down one word for each of the following phrases.

(a) Full of rest

(b) Full of harm

(c) Full of grace

(d) Full of joy

(e) Full of fear

(f) Full of care

(g) Full of wonder

(h) If you have as much as you can carry in your arms, it's an ....

(i) If you have as much as you can hold in your hand, it's a ....

(j) If a cup is full to the brim, it's ....

5 Go bush

The 'bush' below displays a single, trunk-like word, EUCALYPTUS. See if you can cause the bush to branch out properly by filling the spaces with words from the list.

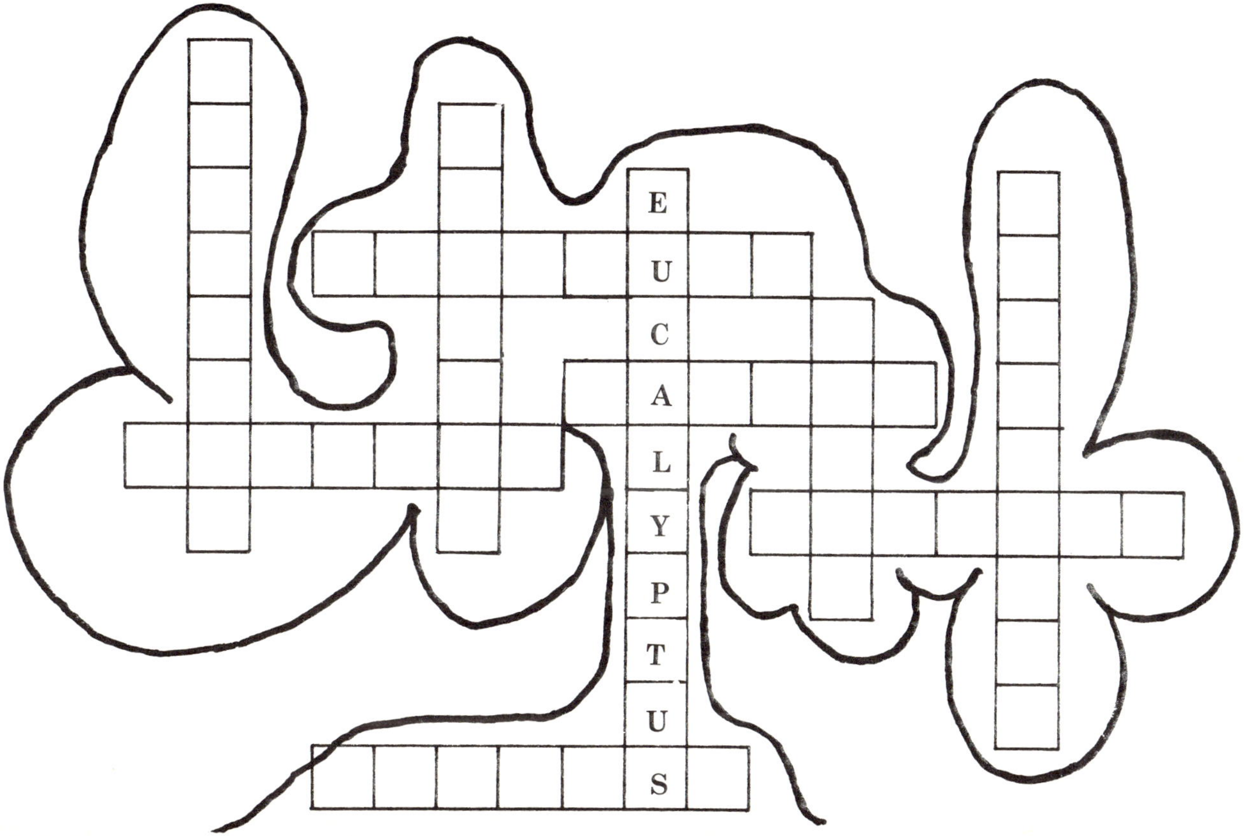

6 Solve the word equations

Using the letters arranged in mathematical form, write down the list words they represent.

(a) 2L+2V+E=

(b) 2A+2N+TUB+D=

(c) 2T+2E+CUL=

(d) 2N+FAT+OUI=

(e) 2E+2R+DAN+G=

(f) 30+2S+PIN+U=

7 Petals

Pairs of words from the list are flowering below. Two letters from each word appear in the centre of each 'flower'. Find both words.

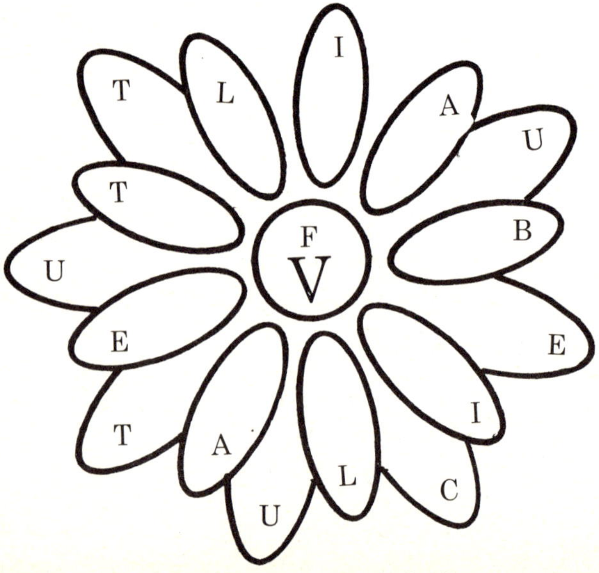

26 MATHS

calculate	subtraction
division	bisect
addition	degree
multiply	numeral
remainder	radius
brackets	circumference
equation	decimal
diameter	positive
problem	negative
parallel	graph

1 Jumbled equations

Find list words by solving the following equations and unjumbling the letters.

21+yum+pit=llyumpit=multiply

(a) tngavi+2e=?

(b) mid+ce+la=?

(c) 4e+4c+3r+nfmui—ecr=?

(d) per+3l+2a=?

(e) lunar+module—ludo=?

(f) drink+emerald—kdl=?

(g) 2(c+l+a)+ute=?

(h) nose+video+2i—2e—o=?

2 Use the clues!

Use each of the following clues to identify a word from the list.

(a) Begins with a confused mare.

(b) Without the first and last letters you have a loud noise.

(c) Has a confused free near its end.

(d) Ends late.

(e) To steal after the first letter.

(f) Ends with a religious group that has split from the main church.

(g) Last four letters plus the first gives one of the seven deadly sins.

(h) Slosson Intelligence Test (*inits.*) in the middle.

(i) A large public transport vehicle in reverse to start.

(j) The end is sight.

3 Symbols

Find the list words suggested by each of the following symbols.

(a) [ ]

(b)

(c) —

(d) x

(e) + (2 words)

(f) — (2 words)

(g) (3 words)

(h) ═════

(i) 2x+3y=z

(j) 45°

4 Thirds

Every third letter of the following list words is provided. Work out the remaining letters and so identify the words.

(a) _ _u_ _i_ _

(b) _ _m_ _a_

(c) _ _c_ _a_

(d) _ _m_ _n_ _r

(e) _ _l_ _l_ _e

(f) _ _r_ _l_ _

(g) _ _s_ _t

(h) _ _s_ _i_ _

(i) _ _r_ _m_ _r_ _c_

5 Syllable jumble

By choosing one correct syllable from each column and rearranging them, identify the following list words.

(a)	ply	trac	par
(b)	it	ga	tion
(c)	lel	pos	sub
(d)	e	re	di
(e)	main	qua	tive
(f)	tion	al	ive
(g)	ne	sion	ti
(h)	vi	mul	der

6 Star-words

Each of the following star-words contains four list words with a common letter in the middle. By using one letter for each space along the lines (starting from the number each time), and using the letters already provided, find the words that fill out each star. (One word is already done in the first star.)

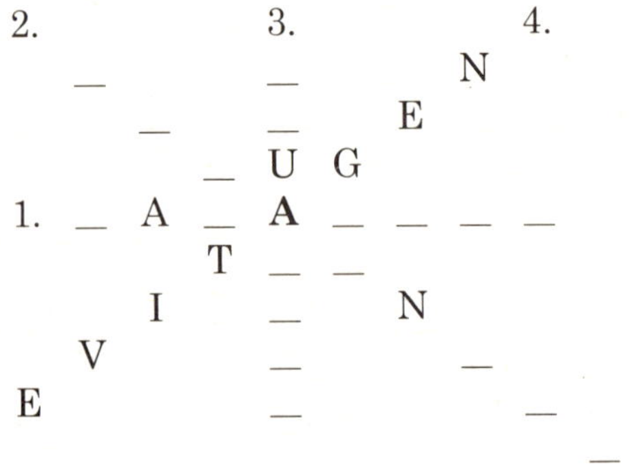

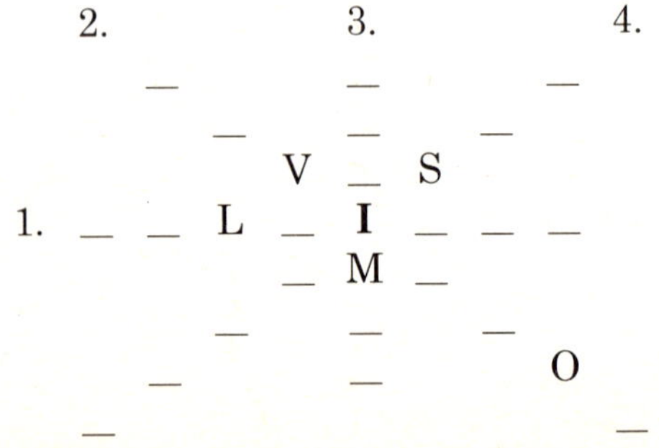

7 Sentence jumble

Re-arrange the words in each of the following groups, and so create sentences each with a list word correctly used.

(a) to the able were problem solve you?

(b) each to road the and ran line other railway the parallel.

(c) nearby remainder the the visited island a passengers of.

(d) was it car the positive that right witness was the.

(e) part brackets you of to calculate in first have the which the the is equation.

27 SCIENTIFICALLY SPEAKING

dissolve	experiment
chemical	gases
evaporate	absorb
thermometer	produce
liquid	theory
diagram	fluid
oxygen	crystal
dilute	gravity
density	laboratory
expansion	solution

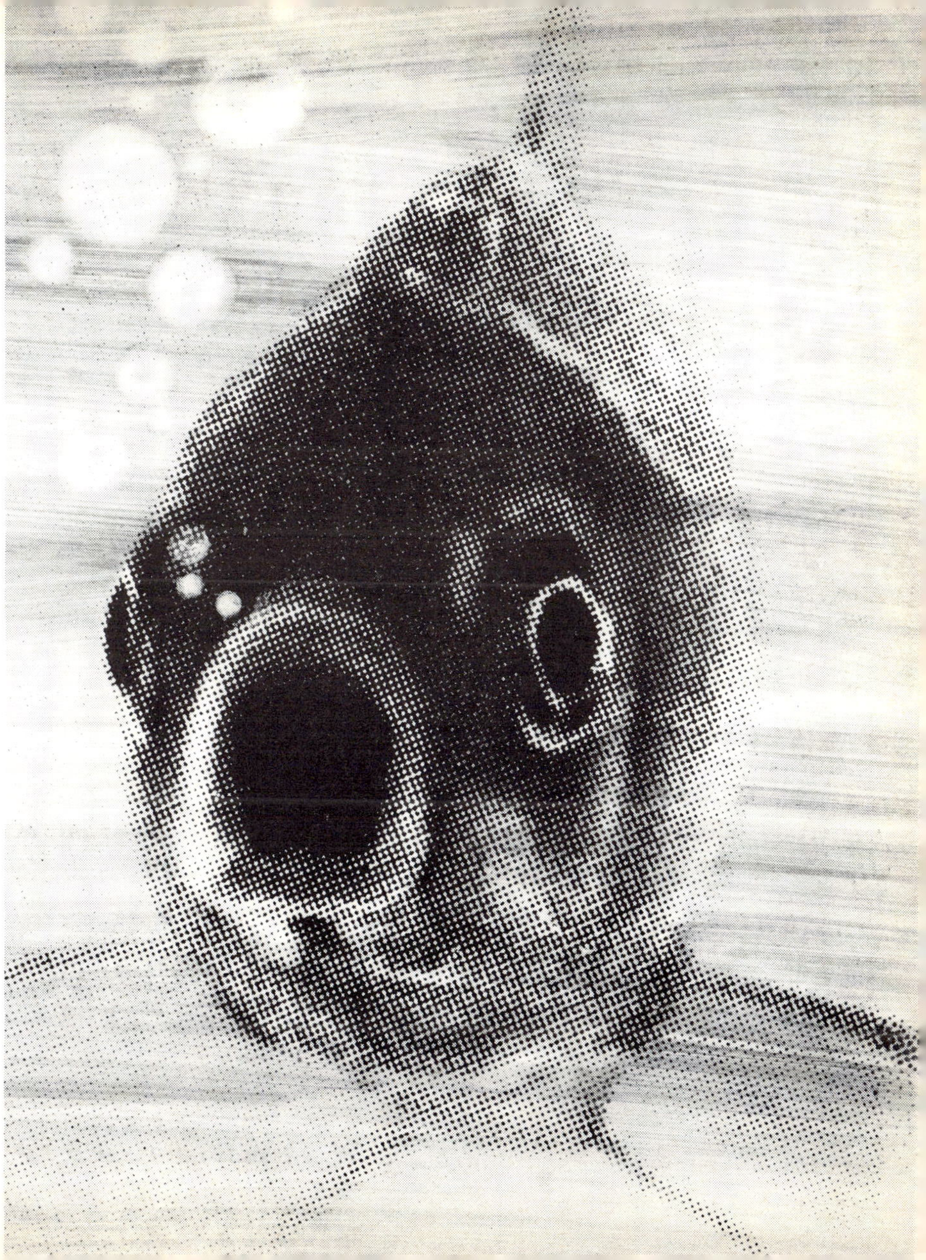

1 Clues

Work out the list words by using the clues.

(a) This word has a nasty rodent in it.

(b) This word has a mother in the middle of it.

(c) This word has x and y but not z.

(d) This word ends with a male sheep.

(e) This word ends with an abbreviation for Allan.

(f) This word has the plural of man in it.

(g) This word rhymes with gravity.

(h) Babies often do the beginning of this word.

(i) This word rhymes with 'assassinate'.

(j) This word rhymes with 'revolve'.

2 Sciencegrams

Read the riddle, ponder the clue,
then rearrange the letters
till it dawns on you.
In short, find the list word!

Out, out, out!
Getting bigger and bigger
And, sometimes, thinner and thinner.
PINAXONES

With sharp edges
And regular sides,
This often appears
When a substance subsides.
TLYCARS

Up, up, and away!
Gone in far less than a day
In a most invisible way.
VIDSLOSE

You've got quite a grip
On us it seems,
But, rather than grapple,
I'll settle for an apple.
RATYGIV

Very mental,
Hardly ever sentimental,
Other scientists lend an ear—
That's the idea!
RHYETO

Full of tubes
And bottles and lenses
And stains and smells
And full-length benches.
TAYBALRORO

3 Rising to the occasion

Science uses curves to illustrate experiments. Here's a word curve that's formed by using some science words. Find the words using the clues given. *Note:* You may first of all have to sort out the clues themselves!

CLUES

11. A non-solid and a gas.
22. Another word for 'give' and mass per unit of volume.
33. A substance that can usually react with other substances and a liquid with something dissolved in it.
44. To turn into vapour and a spreading out, e.g. of a gas.
55. The place where theories are tested and the name of such a test.
6. An instrument for measuring the degree of heat or cold.

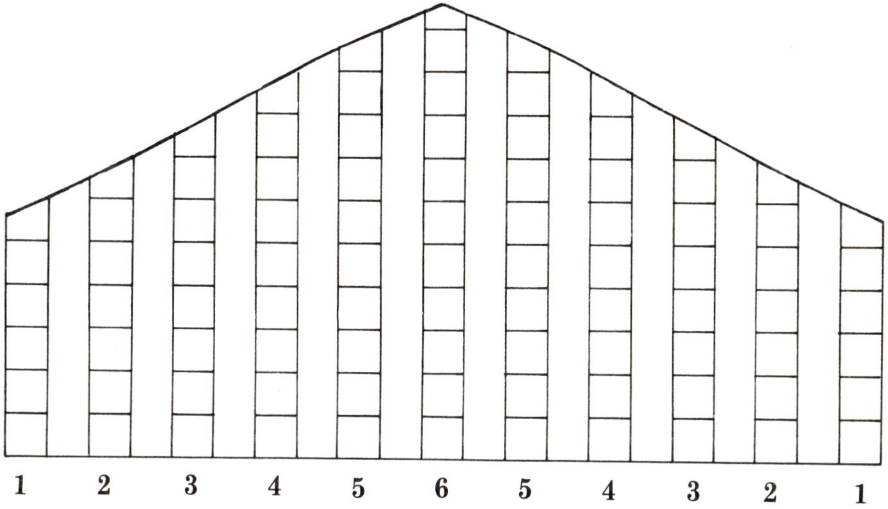

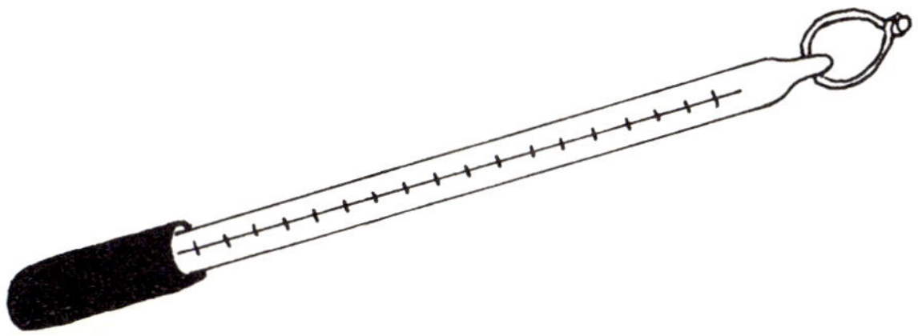

4 Funnels

Funnel in the correct form of the list word that will make sense in each of the sentences below.

(a) The substance was tested to make sure it was ___ pure.

chemically / chemistry / chemical

(b) The apparatus was described and a ___ representation was also supplied.

diagram / diagrammatic / diagrammatically

(c) The scientist was careful to add that his views were still only ___

theory / theoretically / theoretical

oxygenated / oxygenate / oxygen

(d) Blood is ___ by the lungs.

(e) In cross-section the rock was shown to have a ___ structure.

crystallize / crystal / crystalline

(f) The scientific discovery was designed to ___ solids.

liquidity / liquid / liquefy

(g) The development of programmed robot helpers is still at an ___ stage.

experimentally / experimental / experiment

expansion / expanded / expand

(h) Helium is used to ___ weather balloons.

(i) ___ occurs when water is heated.

evaporate / evaporation

dilution / dilute / diluted

(j) Acids often have to be ___ before they can be used ___

experiment / experimental / experimentally

5 Repeats

Quite a few list words repeat a letter in their spelling. As you find such words, fit them into the table below. The first word is done as an example. (*Note:* Some words will fit into more than one place in the table.)

LETTER	WORD
2 B's	Absorb
2 C's	
2 A's	
2 N's	
2 O's	
2 R's	
2 M's	
2 I's	
2 S's	
2 T's	
3 E's	

6 Scientific sentence

Look at this sentence:

> Gustav liked to work by night on his design of some scientific apparatus.

Surprisingly, this sentence contains all the letters needed to make over *fifteen* list words.
AIM: Find over fifteen list words.
METHOD: No holds barred. Choose letters from anywhere and use any letter as many times as you like.
EXAMPLE: **dilute**

Now you're on your own!

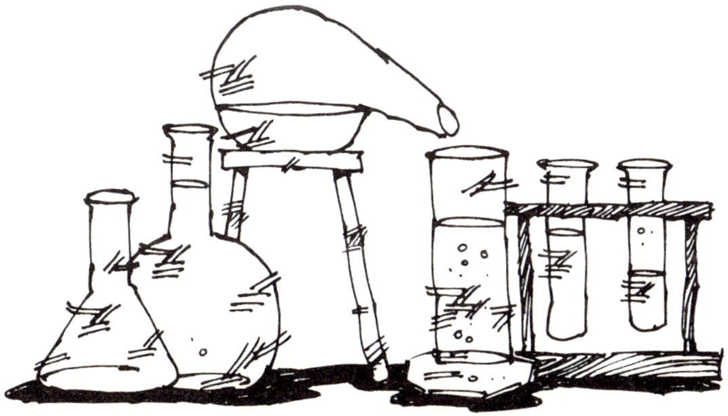

7 Atoms

Each of the 'atoms' below contains two words from the list. The 'nucleus' in the centre of each atom gives you four letters. Add letters from the outer shell to those in the nucleus to form the two list words.

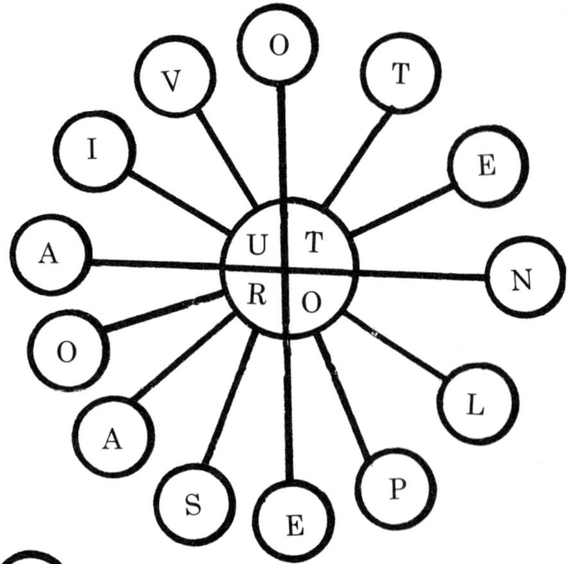

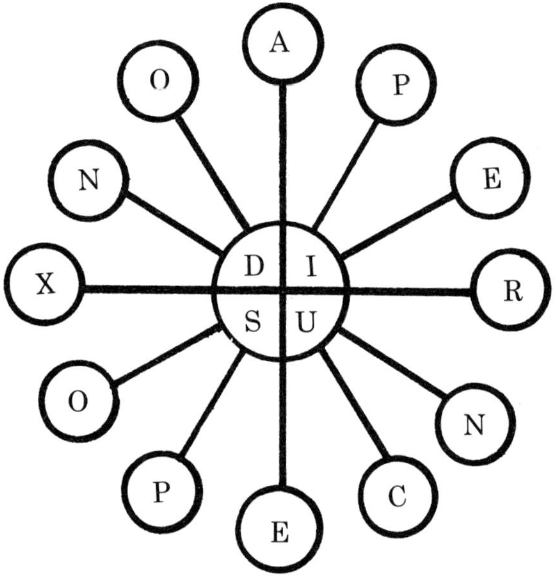

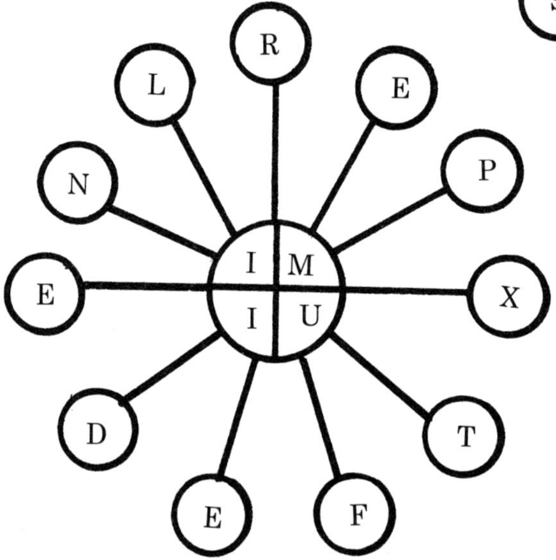

recent	again
during	monthly
before	daily
yesterday	yearly
often	future
morning	autumn
evening	already
early	o'clock
occasion	frequent
moment	previous

28 NOW, THEN, SOON

1

Fill in words from your list to make sensible sentences.

(a) Many pupils arrive e............ at school every m............ .

(b) Y............ my brother fell over and broke his arm.

(c) B............ I do my homework, I switch off the television.

(d) There are a number of m............ magazines which appeal to teenagers.

(e) Our y............ exams are usually in November.

(f) The milkman delivers our milk about 5 o............ each morning.

2 Jumbled words

Hidden in the following table are eight of your list words. They occur in a straight line horizontally, vertically or diagonally, and some will read back-to-front.

N	O	I	S	A	C	C	O
E	D	D	A	D	F	Y	Q
T	A	L	R	E	A	D	Y
F	I	R	B	U	U	U	U
O	L	G	L	C	T	R	E
H	Y	T	H	Y	U	I	I
M	K	N	O	W	M	N	O
T	A	G	A	I	N	G	U

3 Mix and match

Write down the words from the left-hand column. Then match them up with the correct ending from the right-hand column.

(a)	month	ious
(b)	dail	ent
(c)	prev	y
(d)	aut	ure
(e)	mom	ly
(f)	be	ing
(g)	dur	umn
(h)	fut	fore

4 Cracking the code

Take the shape formed by the lines around the letter as a code.

a	e	i
d	g	n
y	l	r

Now decode the following list words.

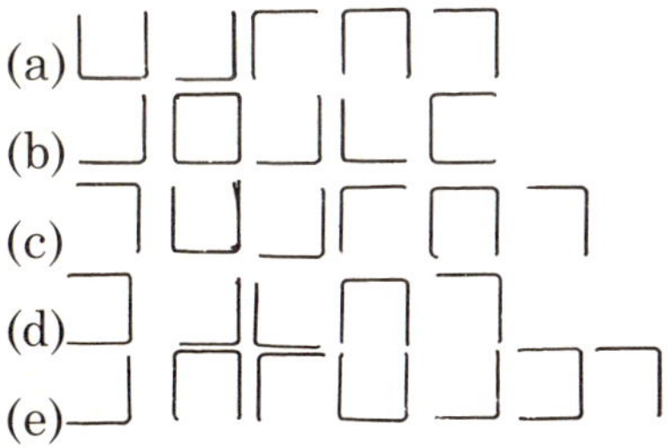

5 ABC

Six of the list words end with a 'y'. Arrange them in alphabetical order.

6 Guessing game

The last two letters of list words are given below. Write down the words.

(a) ay (b) on
(c) mn (d) ck
(e) en (f) in
(g) dy (h) us

7 Scrambled words

Unscramble the letters to form list words.

(a) vinegen (b) necter
(c) queenrtf (d) tommen
(e) ccsoonia (f) dryysatee
(g) niaga (h) soupvire

29 In Defence

soldier	missile
military	prisoner
lieutenant	surround
enemy	abandon
parachute	superior
bullet	oppose
courage	surrender
ammunition	defence
buried	sergeant
battle	nuclear

1 Double march

Some words in the list have double letters. See if you can take such words in your stride by filling in the spaces below to form list words with double letters. The double letters in each word are indicated by numbers equivalent to the letters in the alphabet (e.g. A=1).

(a) __ 18 18 _____

(b) __ 12 12 __

(c) _ 13 13 ________

(d) __ 20 20 __

(e) __ 18 18 ______

(f) _ 16 16 ___

(g) _ 19 19 ___

2 Victory words

Below are three list word 'armies', A, B and C. Other words can be formed within each 'army'. These are your victory words. The army that gains the greatest point score for its quota of 'victory words' is the winner.

Example: 'Neat' can be formed from the letters in the first four words of A. 'Ape' can be formed from words 2, 3 and 4 of B.

Scoring: 'Neat' is worth 4; 'Ape' is worth 3. A 5-letter word would be worth 5, and so on.

Note: Build words only from left to right.

ARMY A				
1	2	3	4	5
S	C	N	M	S
U	O	U	I	U
R	U	C	L	R
R	R	L	I	R
O	A	E	T	E
U	G	A	A	N
N	E	R	R	D
D			Y	E
				R

ARMY B				
1	2	3	4	5
P	A	S	B	S
A	B	U	U	E
R	A	P	R	A
A	N	E	I	R
C	D	R	E	G
H	O	I	D	E
U	N	O		A
T		R		N
E				T

ARMY C				
1	2	3	4	5
P	D	M	L	A
R	E	I	I	M
I	F	S	E	M
S	E	S	U	U
O	N	I	T	N
N	C	L	E	I
E	E	E	N	T
R			A	I
			N	O
			T	N

3 Words at the ready

The words gathered in the 'barracks' below are simply awaiting the opportunity to fill the gaps in the sentences. Note that the different forms (or parts of speech of a word) belong with one or other of the groups of sentences.

superior superiority	courageous courageously courage
bury buried burial	defence defensive defender defend

(a) The .... forces are trained to take up .... positions in time of attack.

Each soldier as a .... is expected to .... his or her country against aggression.

(b) A soldier is expected to show .... and be able to act .... in an emergency.

The more desperate the emergency, the more .... a soldier should be.

(c) In peacetime, live ammunition is sometimes ....

It is possible to .... live ammunition and recover it later provided that both the .... and the recovery are performed with great care.

(d) A soldier is expected to obey a .... officer.

This idea of .... and obedience is common to every army.

4 Flag raiser

Both flag and battlements are raised on list words. Try sorting them out. (Note: Each word in the battlements extends itself by one letter.)

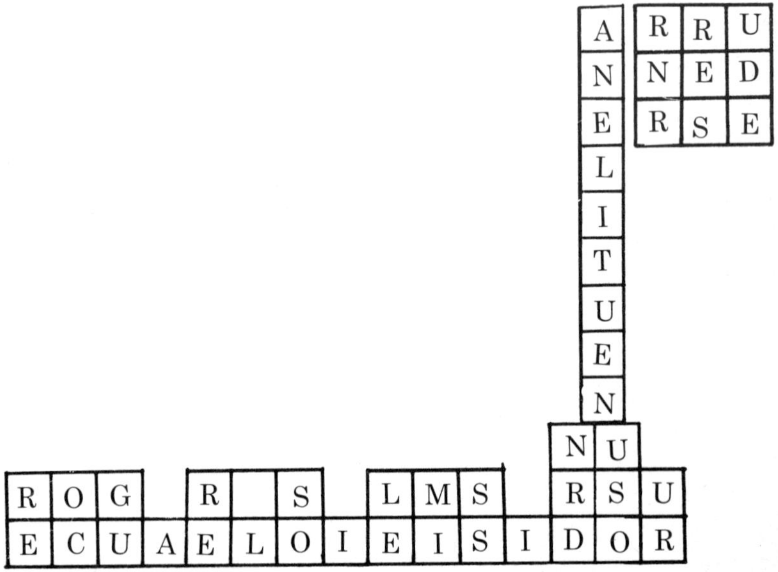

5 Where words come from

Soldier

The word 'soldier' owes its origin to the way the Roman soldiers were paid. They were paid with a Roman coin called a *solidus* which meant, as the word suggests, 'something solid'.

-pose comes from the Latin word *pono* (*positum*) which means to 'place or put'. Fill in the -pose words and try to write down their meanings.

(a) _mpose
(b) c_mpose
(c) r_pose
(d) s_p_ose
(e) _epose
(f) t_a_spose
(g) super_mpose
(h) e_pose
(i) pr_pose
(j) d__pose
(k) i_t_rpose

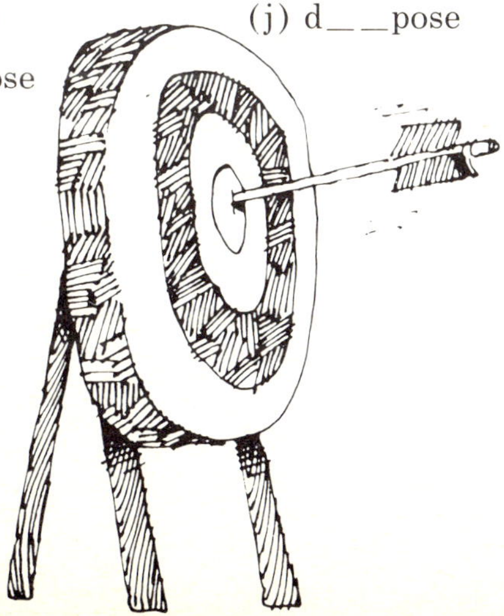

6 On target

Each list word in Ring 1 has a synonym (or word with a similar meaning) in Ring 2 and an antonym (or word with an opposite meaning) in Ring 3. Find the correct synonym and antonym for each list word. (*Note:* There is one list word used that has, for its antonym, another list word.)

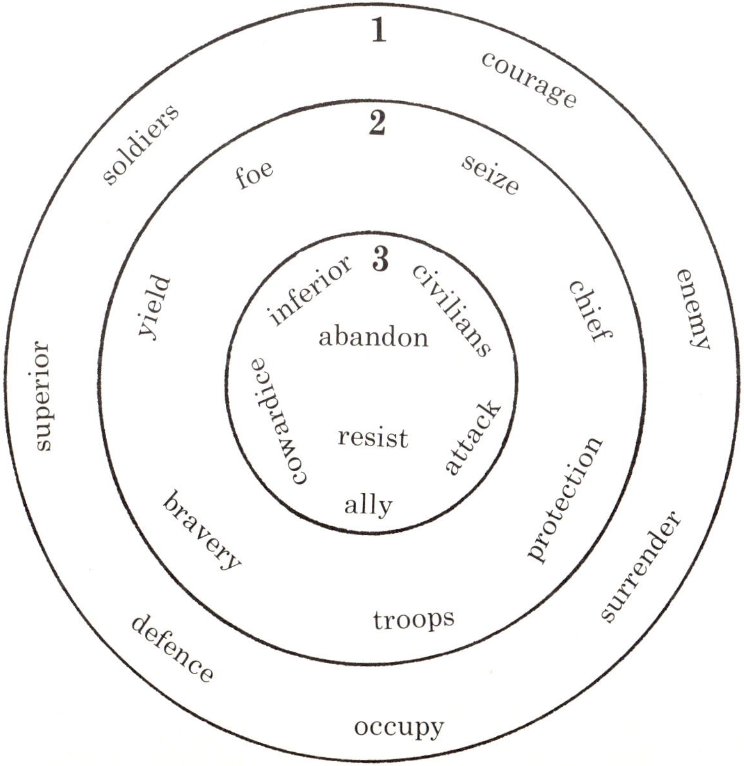

7 Stripes

Some of your list words contain tricky letter combinations that can throw you when you're doing your best to spell a word. So, promote yourself by getting in amongst the stripes below and fitting the rest of each list word round its trickiest letters.

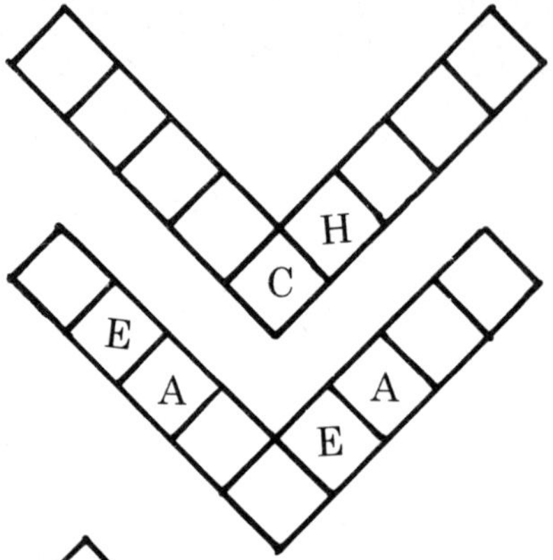

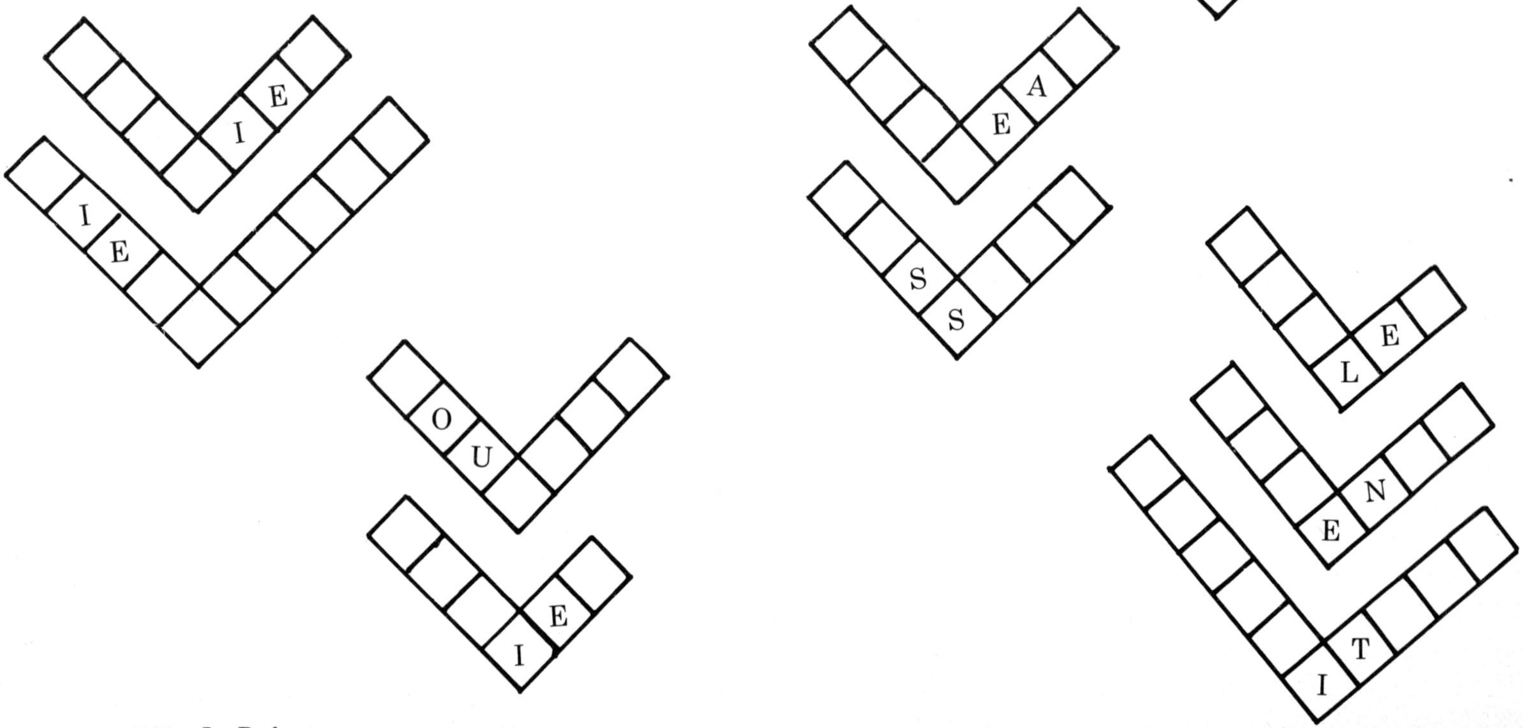

piano	harmony
keyboard	percussion
soloist	conductor
tone	guitar
drummer	trombone
rhythm	orchestra
organ	group
vocal	lyrics
melody	compose
trumpet	microphone

30 In the Groove

1 Word clues

Use these clues to help you find words from your list.

(a) Begins with a kind of hurt.

(b) Ends with a pet.

(c) Has a backwards sop in it.

(d) A jumbled note.

(e) Ends with a backwards rot.

(f) Name of a fish.

(g) Ends with a backwards rat.

(h) Has a backward nob in it.

(i) Ends with a backwards nag.

(j) Has a chest in the middle.

2 Matching word and meaning

Find list words from column A to match the meanings in column B. The first one is done for you.

	COLUMN A	COLUMN B
(a)	guitar	a stringed instrument
(b)	....	quality of musical sound
(c)	....	words of a song
(d)	....	leader of an orchestra or band
(e)	....	instrument for picking up sound
(f)	....	to write music
(g)	....	a tune
(h)	....	a group of instruments
(i)	....	an electronic keyboard instrument
(j)	....	the beat of the music

3 ABC

Arrange the following list words in the order in which they would occur in the dictionary.

rhythm	melody
percussion	soloist
compose	microphone
drummer	piano
keyboard	trombone

4

Copy the diagram into your workbooks. Then arrange all the words from the list under the appropriate heading. For example, 'trumpet' would go under the heading, 'To Do With an Instrument', and 'vocal' would go under the heading 'To Do With Voice'. Some list words will go under both headings — e.g. soloist. Position the remaining list words appropriately.

To Do With an Instrument	To Do With Voice

5 Secret code

Solve the secret code to find these list words. Your only clue is that in this code, 'piano' would be written 'qjbop'.

wpdbm	dpoevdups	mzsjdt	upof
pshbo	psdiftusb	qfsdvttjpo	

6 Free composition

Use the following list words as base words and see how many other words you can create by using only the letters contained in each word. The first list has been started for you to give you the idea.

MICROPHONE	ORCHESTRA
phone one more	

7 Word salad

In the word salad, twelve words from the list are hidden. They may be written forwards or backwards, up or down (but *not* diagonally). Find the twelve words.

N	S	G	X	U	A	N	T	Z	R	P	H	E
O	T	R	U	M	P	E	T	A	S	B	L	G
A	S	O	T	O	Y	N	L	P	C	J	K	N
Z	B	U	J	I	S	O	L	O	I	S	T	H
A	A	P	W	M	H	T	Y	H	R	C	D	C
G	L	L	Y	I	A	X	N	D	Y	C	E	F
M	K	A	S	B	R	V	M	E	L	O	D	Y
I	F	C	C	O	M	P	O	S	E	R	E	D
E	N	O	B	M	O	R	T	O	L	G	B	K
R	S	V	S	Q	N	R	O	P	I	A	N	O
T	E	V	S	P	Y	P	J	Y	F	N	A	Z
U	U	I	W	H	X	L	Q	G	M	N	J	N

Index

The bold numerals refer to units.